GN00983350

Diggers & Dreamers

2004/2005

Edited by

Sarah Bunker   Christine Charnock

Chris Coates   David Hodgson

Jonathan How

DIGGERS AND DREAMERS PUBLICATIONS

©
**Diggers & Dreamers
Publications
2003**

First published
2003
D&D Publications
BCM Edge
London
WC1N 3XX

ISBN
0 9545757 0 9
Paperback

Distribution
Edge of Time Ltd
BCM Edge
London
WC1N 3XX
(07000) 780536

Printing (contents)
Greenwood Recycled
Printing
(01484) 844841

Printing (cover)
Buckingham Colour
Press
(01280) 824000

Typesetting and Layout
Jonathan How
(0870) 4442566
Sarah Bunker
(01363) 877228

All rights reserved. No part of this book may be reproduced for purposes of resale or publication without written permission from the publisher, except by a reviewer who may quote brief passages or reproduce illustrations in a review; nor may any part of this book be stored in a retrieval system, or transmitted in any form or by any means electronic, mechanical, photocopying, recording, or other, without written permission from the publisher, unless the information so stored and retrieved is made available to the public entirely free of charge (meaning that no joining fees, user fees, handling fees, nor access fees may be charged).

However, it is our intent and desire that the information contained in the Guide be made as widely available as possible; therefore, we grant permission to organisations that are strictly non-profit making to republish excerpts, provided that the combined length of such excerpts does not exceed 1,000 words, and also provided that each excerpt is accompanied by the credit line: "Reprinted with permission from Diggers and Dreamers 2004/2005".

Furthermore, we grant permission to private individuals to reproduce and distribute this information among friends and acquaintances, as long as the nature of the exchange is non-commercial and the information is provided free of charge save for reimbursement of copying and mailing expenses.

Acknowledgements: Thank you to all the communities, housing co-ops and other organisations that have responded to our requests for information. Once again we've been to several places for our meetings in the last two years, so grateful thanks to everyone at Old Hall, Laurieston, Bamford, The Community Project and Redfield for being such generous hosts.

INTRODUCTION

Since we launched our website in 2001 we seem to have been inundated with TV companies trying to get their cameras inside a communal household — whether they want to make the latest reality TV show — 'BIG COMMUNE!' / 'I Share a House With 10 Other People — Get Me Out of Here!', or an in-depth look at communal living at the dawn of the 21st Century, their chances of getting over the communal doorstep are practically zero. The only way you will find out about communal lifestyles is to visit and try them for yourself.

It could be argued that more people than ever before are seeking communal solutions to their lifestyles. New directions have started to emerge over the past few years; an older generation looking for models of communal living, like Cohousing, that might offer an alternative to institutional homes, or later-life isolation. A younger generation, radicalised by Anti-Road/Globalisation protests are looking to Low-Impact Living and Permaculture in search of sustainable lifestyles. Set this alongside the 'communes' and primary focus (Spiritual/Social) communities that have 'survived' from the supposed 1970's 'heyday' of communal living and perhaps — just perhaps — there is a resurgence of communal living starting to happen!

Diggers & Dreamers continues to chronicle the comings and goings of communal living in the UK through its directory and complimentary publications and website — **www.diggersanddreamers.org.uk**

10 Myths of Communal Living

1. There is a leader really, isn't there?

Some communities have true leaders (esp. religious communities) and hierarchies, which may be influenced by the length of time a person has lived in the community. Sometimes there is a perceived 'leadership' which truly only exists within the mind of the newest person or people. Certainly, knowledge is power and anyone who has lived in community for any length of time can confirm that the most efficient way of dispelling this myth is to share information and skills freely. This may be easier said than done as there will always be new members who are happy to rely on the more experienced people while they find their feet.

Group dynamics plays a significant role as the loudest person may be perceived as being 'in charge', although this is most certainly not the case and you will find if you pry a little deeper that they get away with it because no-one can be bothered to challenge them any more and that their views, though vociferously expressed, are generally not the dominant views. In every group there will be natural leaders, instigators of serious work or serious fun and each individual has the opportunity to discover his/her own strengths. It is no shame to realise that you should take a back seat sometimes and put your trust in the judgement of the people you have chosen to live with.

Power can sometimes be wielded in a negative way

when individuals choose to withhold information for their own purposes. The most likely time for this to occur is when there are split loyalties in the community and, if you witness this in a place you are thinking of joining, you may be advised to wait until the 'storming' is over before you commit.

There is sometimes a strong anti-leadership culture in community, once referred to as the 'Tyrany of Structurelessness.' True anarchy? That could be disputed. This type of social arrangement can be quite destructive as communication breaks down, followed by lack of trust and possibly the demise of the communal group. The things you need most of all to develop as a group are mutual trust and respect. Once those have gone there is no turning back.

Another occasion when you might encounter this is when someone decides to use their power of veto, effectively blocking community decision making. Again, the key issue is trust and you must trust that they do not have alterior motives.

It is possible — and indeed necessary in large groups — to devolve responsibility for decision making to 'sub-committees,' as in the case of Twin Oaks in America and other larger communities where it would be tiresome, cumbersome and maybe downright impossible to involve everyone in all decision-making.

Non-communards often find it difficult to believe that we do get things done without anyone being in charge, but, believe me when I say that trying to be the 'leader' in the midst of a group of strong-minded, educated, opinionated communards is not a position anyone would take on willingly!

2. Community living will save my relationship

If you go into communal life hoping for a 'quick fix' of your failing relationship, you are more than likely consigning it to the grave. Living in community highlights all of your personal foibles and failings (as well as your strengths) and your unsatisfactory relationship will probably be revealed for what it is. If you have been fooling yourself, better watch out! On the other hand, if you see your partner in a new light as he/she develops within the group, you may find yourselves growing closer. You have to work harder at keeping intimate relationships active and strong as they are in competition with the other relationships you will develop within the community.

3. You don't eat meat or smoke, do you?

You may be surprised to discover that communities are full of normal people, with normal desires and failings. So, yes, there are smokers and omnivores and all other sectors of the population are also represented therein.

In order to be able to live happily in a mixed, non-idealistic community you will have to come to terms with this fact. If you want a vegan, non-smoking environment, then there are communities that will cater for your needs. Internal agreements about how, when and where you do something that might be considered controversial within your group, like smoking in communal areas, will be discussed and decided within your group, just as it would be within your family home.

If you have special needs because of a medical problem, your chosen community will accommodate them or will advise you that they can't continue with your membership application. This does not mean that unforeseen disagreements on moral or ethical matters will never arise and being accepted into a community is an expression of a mutual desire to develop an honest and open relationship with your fellow communards. So, if you know there is an issue you will never compromise on, ask before you join.

Psst — wanna share a can of tuna?

4. So now I'll have time to be creative...

Maybe, when the work is all done, which is usually never! Community maintenance is akin to painting the Forth Bridge. If you are good at time management, can juggle your community commitments (2 days a week

The children's first willow sculpture seemed a little ambitious....

equivalent?), have an understanding family and a regular source of income then you may have time to spend on your own projects.

You could choose to channel your creative talents into community projects and enhance the place you live in. An arbour in the garden, a sculpture in the hallway, a beautiful flower border or cooking sumptuous meals, will all be appreciated. It can be difficult to find quality time for yourself but you must do it otherwise you will come to resent the 'demands' the community 'makes on you' and that unfulfilled feeling will be your downfall.

It is finding the balance between communal life and 'having a life' that can be difficult.

5. But I CAME to community for shared childcare!

You simply can't assume other adults will be responsible for your kids and will need to make clear arrangements, both with other parents and non-parents. Community kids tend to hang out in packs but do not assume that it is acceptable to add yours to the mix and abandon them to their fate. However loose an arrangement seems, there will always be someone who is responsible for the children and you need to liase with them. You will also be required to be that person when it is your 'turn.'

Communities can be great places for children to grow up in and they do it very quickly! They have a selection of 'parent figures' to take their troubles to and who will be keen to develop mutual interests. They soon develop a sense of who they are in the midst of it all and become confident young people. In fact, parents often complain that they lose their children when they move in as they have so many exciting things to do that they forget that they have parents.

There will also be as many different ways of parenting as there are parents. Don't assume that everyone holds the same opinions as you. Sharing childcare can be one of the most controversial aspects of communal living. We each have our own ideas about discipline, mealtimes, cleanliness, respect for others and for the property of others. . . the list is endless.

Sharing your space with home-educated

children can cause conflict if you choose to send your kids to school and need to follow a fixed routine. Unless they adore going to school, there may be a few arguments about bedtime and the exciting things that Georgina gets to do while they have to spend all day cooped up in a classroom.

Talk it through with the parents in the community and establish where your personal tolerance levels lie. It can be extremely rewarding to have the opportunity to develop relationships with children other than your own (for you and the children concerned) or, if you have chosen not to have children, to build those relationships if you want to and enjoy a child's perspective of the world.

6. Peace, man

Not all communities are politically motivated in the sense of taking direct action. However, choosing to live your life in this way is a political statement in itself and is a fairly radical choice to make. Don't be too hard on your hosts if they do not live up to your ideals. They are also living with contradictions, brought about by financial or family constraints. Not everyone wants to live in a bender and eat rabbits. At least they are making an effort and at most they are hoping to make an impact on the minds and opinions of others by being open to sharing their home and being a living example of an alternative existence. People living there will generally be very supportive of political action and sometimes quite left-wing in their opinions.

Things may have felt more 'radical' in the

'old days' of 'hippie communes', but where are they today? Many existing communities owe their current stability to sound financial management and the interpersonal skills of their members. There are still radical, front-line people out there who are committed to wider social or environmental change and if you are seeking that route, try one of the Radical Routes communities.

7. Communities are just a bunch of old hippies

The word 'commune' conjures up images of spaced-out dropouts and 'community' is more generally favoured.

The current trend towards exploring 'down-sizing' attracted many journalists to the existing, successful communities in search of a story. Some of what you may have read may be true. It is all very well for people with high incomes and a better than average standard of living to talk about giving it all up in favour of communal living, especially if they have the safety net of savings or a second home to fall back on if it all goes wrong. For many people, living in community affords them the opportunity to realise their ambitions without having to accrue capital first. It has been a silent revolution, born out of the squatting movement and the old hippie communes of the 60's and carried through by a bunch of dedicated idealists who made the dream real for many people. Living in community is never running away from responsibility, but running towards it with arms (and mind) open.

Collective housing is in vogue at present, recognising some people's need to belong to a wider community and the benefits of co-operation and sharing resources on a larger scale. Eco-villages are sprouting up but are only accessible to those with capital and income, unless you choose to take the low impact living route and buy land to live on in tipis or benders. These can be very beautiful buildings, but the local planning office may not be sympathetic.

8. One big mattress

Just like the real world, everyone else seems to be getting your share! Some communities

(Atlantis, Zegg, Kerista, Tamera) have experimented with the idea of open relationships, but it is a tough road to follow. Free sex? - nope, you have to pay for it as much as everywhere else, at least on an emotional level. Affairs within the community are difficult to conceal and although you will certainly develop close personal relationships with people, you have the opportunity to do this without the distraction of a sexual relationship developing if you choose to do so. There is likely to be more sexual intrigue in your local, wider community than in the house you all live in. There may be a bit of 'partner swapping' every now and then when relationships break down and new ones form but this is more likely to take the form of serial monogamy than a 'free for all.'

9. So I can just forget about money, right?

Nice try. No, you still need to be aware of sources of income (especially your own!) and, to a certain extent, where it all goes. If you take on the role of treasurer for your group, you will become intimately familiar with all of the financial ups and downs of community life.

Communities vary in their choice of financial structure. You will find some that are able to house you for a monthly rent payment, others that require you to buy in, take out a

Yes... the communal cash tins really WERE multiplying

mortgage or pay some kind of loan stock as a financial commitment to the community.

If your group has a Treasurer, you will be relieved of the tedium of actually paying bills and making the bank statement balance. Your commitment is to pay up regularly and not to take it all for granted. Being heavily in debt without the consent of your fellow communards is likely to result in your being shown the door. Never assume you can go into debt.

In some communities, the cost of buying your unit can be as much as £170,000. In others, all you need is a couple of hundred each month. It can be a very inexpensive way to live, but don't forget you are paying for that by committing your time and energy as well as your money.

Income-sharing or -pooling communities also exist. They often require a greater personal time commitment. Radical Routes communities expect members to have a commitment to social change.

10. I will get all the support I need from living in a community.

And so, the last myth explodes. Sorry, communities are generally not the place to go for therapy, unless that is their stated aim. In order to function well within the community, you will need to be a fairly strong person, aware of your own needs and capable of self-expression. That doesn't mean that we are perfect all of the time; we all have our 'wobbly' days when we will be offered help and support to get us through. However, if you know you will need much more than the occasional hug, choose your community with care. It's not that people don't care, rather there is so much to be aware of that it is easy to misinterpret someone's moods, or simply not notice.

As a single person in a couple-oriented community, you are quite likely to feel lonely unless you make the effort and develop your own social life. Other people are not going to do it for you. On the other hand, living with lots of people does give you the opportunity to join in with whatever is going on, to learn new skills and you will (probably) never have to go to the cinema alone again (unless you want to)...

DIRECTORY OF COMMUNITIES AND NETWORKS

ABOUT THIS DIRECTORY

In the Directory we list existing and embryonic UK communities and Networks which have chosen to have entries. As you will see when you start to read their entries, there is a wide variety of types of communal living groups; some of these groups may work together, some may income share, some may have a spiritual focus, some may not necessarily live under the same roof; whole groups, or people within the groups, may be committed to ideals such as permaculture, veganism, home education and struggling against sexism, racism and homophobia; others may well not.

Remember that there are many other communal groups who are not listed, including countless shared houses, but all the groups in this directory share a desire to be public about their lifestyle; many are looking for new members, and most of them welcome visitors. If you are thinking about living communally and want to experience what these places are like, this is the place to start. If you do decide that you want to visit one or more places then please don't just turn up. Remember that you will be going into people's homes, and it is important to write to them (perhaps letting them know why you are interested) and wait for an invitation to come. Some groups set aside particular dates for welcoming first-time visitors, others welcome volunteers, WWOOFers (Worldwide Opportunities On Organic Farms - address on p 232) or run workshops or courses which may be a good way of visiting for the first time, although you probably won't get a flavour of day-to-day communal life. Don't be shy of visiting, though; most groups rely on a stream of visitors to find the new members that are essential for the ongoing life of the community, and a wealth of experiences awaits you!

HOW TO USE THE INDEX, MAP AND DIRECTORY

The Index at the back of the book is intended to help you select the groups you may wish to visit. We have tried, as far as possible, to go by groups' own answers to the questions. A ◆ is only shown if their answer was definitely "yes". If their answer was "no" or ambiguous then nothing is shown. In such cases it might mean, for example, that they do income share in some way or that they do eat communally occasionally. Where a group's diet is shown as vegetarian (vtn) it means that they never consume any meat (although there's often some ambiguity around fish); and where it is vegan (vgn), that they never consume any animal products.

A letter denotes those communities with a spiritual focus:

A	**Anthroposophy (philosophy of Rudolf Steiner)**
B	**Buddhist**
C	**Christian**
H	**Hindu**
Q	**Quaker**
S	**Spiritual but non-specific**
N	**None**

The numbers on both the index and the map refer to the page number of each group's entry (a few communities did not wish to be shown on the map). Entries are ordered alphabetically.

In the index the column heading 'open in principle' means that the community in question is open to new members in principle, although there might not be space for new members at present. Names are somewhat abridged in the index.

Some groups did not wish their telephone numbers to be published. Some groups did not want their addresses printed; if you write to them 'care of Diggers & Dreamers' we will forward mail directly (unopened) to them. (Our address is at the front of this book.)

Again in this edition are our icons, shown at the bottom of each entry and explained on the next two pages.

DISCLAIMER

The editorial team has always decided that it should trust the groups and allow them to decide, themselves, whether or not they should be included in this directory of communal living. We must point out that we cannot take responsibility for the accuracy of entries, as we are not in a position to verify information sent to us, nor can we be held responsible for anything that may occur to individuals visiting groups as result of reading this directory. Good luck!

DIRECTORY ICONS

We hope that the following icons used in the entries will give you more information — especially about aspects of sustainability. The icons in the embryonic section are in grey since they are aspirations rather than reality.

MONEY

income sharing community-
all income is shared

capital required-
capital required from all members

ENERGY USE

on site electricity generation-
wind, water or solar energy provides some power

solar power used-
solar used for space and/or water heating

insulation to a high standard-
buildings are double-glazed and insulated

TRANSPORT

regular use of bikes for transport

shared use of vehicles-
carpool or recognised arrangements for sharing private cars

easy access to public transport-
bus stop and/or train station within easy walking distance

shared utilities-
domestic facilities (eg washing machines) shared

shared workshop-
communal workshop and communally owned tools

organised recycling system

eco-friendly sewage system-
compost toilets, reed beds or other alternatives in use

LAND, FOOD, SMOKING and ACCESS

land management programme-
members expected to help look after the land

grow a lot of vegetables-
substantial garden (but not necessarily self-sufficient)

animals reared for food-
livestock reared for human consumption

regular communal meals

policy which restricts smoking-
smoking restricted to certain areas or banned

wheelchair access

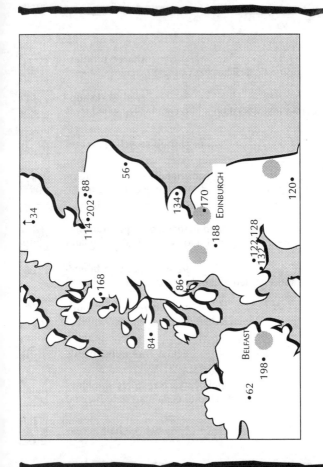

EDINBURGH

BELFAST

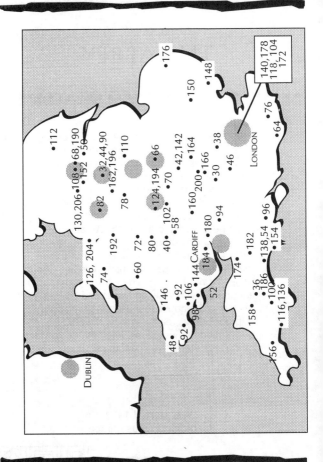

THE ABBEY

T he Abbey is a community and educational /retreat centre, offering possibilities for all who follow a spiritual path, whether or not they come from a particular religious tradition. Our everyday life is based on what we see as the four true relationships to: the Divine, our selves, other people and to the earth. We attempt to live in a way that is simple and ecologically sound and care for a beautiful thirteenth century house. We have regular times for meditation. The Abbey programme provides day and weekend courses related to the above four aspects of relationship, including creative arts, work with body, mind and emotions, interfaith exploration and alternative economics.

Year started 1979
Ideological focus spiritual

The Green, Sutton Courtenay,
Abingdon, Oxfordshire OX14 4AF England
Telephone 01235 847401 **Fax** 01235 847608
Electronic Mail admin@theabbeysc.demon.co.uk
World Wide Web http://www.theabbey.uk.com

The rooms are available for hire; the guest
house accommodates fourteen. There are
four acres of grounds, including an organic
vegetable garden.

ASHRAM COMMUNITY

Ashram Community began in 1967, with the intention of developing committed urban communities, which would develop appropriate new forms of Christian community related to urban needs. This led to having inner-city Community Houses in the 1970's to 1990's, in Rochdale, Middlesborough, London, Sheffield and Birmingham. There are at present two inner-city community houses in Sheffield and one newly opened (2002) in Parkfield, Stockton-on-Tees. Meanwhile, Ashram developed its community presence in terms of shops and residences. The first of these, the Ashram Centre and New Roots Shop (wholefoods, fruit & veg, Traidcraft) was opened in 1987. The second, the Burngreave Ashram and New Roots Shop was opened in 2001. It is a complex of shop, residence, public meeting rooms,

Year started 1967
Ideological focus radical christian

178 Abbeyfield Road,
Sheffield, South Yorkshire S4 7AY England
Telephone 0114 243 6688 **Fax** 0114 244 7278
World Wide Web http://www.ashram.org.uk

offices and basement, plus being the base
for various community groups. It is hoped
that this model of volunteer-served shop
plus local community base plus residence
will develop elsewhere. The shop/house in
the Parkfield inner-city area of Stockton-on-
Tees is on this model. The common life of
Ashram Community is inspired by the radical styles of Jesus and the earliest Christians.
The Community sustains this through
regional Branches, half-yearly Weekends
and half-yearly Community General
Meetings, plus Retreats, Holidays, Walks
and other occasions. In 2001, the
Community wrote and published a
"Discovery Course in Radical Christianity"
called "Journey", which is being used by
groups in many parts of the country.

BALNAKEIL CRAFT VILLAGE

●•●•●•●•●•●•●•●•●•●•●•●•●•●•●•●•

Balnakeil Craft Village was originally built as an early warning station against nuclear attack, but became obsolete before coming fully into use. The site was taken over by the local authority who initiated the craft village, letting the buildings to craftspeople. Later, the buildings were sold to their tenants and they now change hands on the open market. There is no longer any obligation for every building to house a craft business, but a high proportion do so.

The buildings are typical military structures: single-storey, flat-roofed and of concrete block construction. They vary in size, but are mostly roomy enough to contain a shop, workshop and ample family living accom-

Year started 1964
Ideological focus craftwork

Durness, Sutherland IV27 4PT Scotland
Telephone 01971 511296
Electronic Mail michaelbfitch@supanet.com

modation. There are currently about ten
craftshops or galleries, a boatyard and two
restaurants. Another building will be providing a guesthouse. Shops are mostly open
from Spring to October, but one restaurant
is open year-round.

Buildings occasionally come up for sale.
Communal ground includes the village
green and the 'tattie patch', though many
people have individual gardens. There is no
communal organization, but the compact-
ness of the site and the remoteness lead to a
certain feeling of community, the strength of
which inevitably varies from time to time.

BEECH HILL COMMUNITY

We live in a large country house in the rolling Devon hills. Accommodation is both rented and leasehold, in converted outbuildings and in the main house. On our seven acres of land we grow organic fruit and vegetables. We have a paddock with three sheep and chickens, an orchard, a vineyard, a walled garden, a swimming pool, compost toilets and a reed-bed sewage system. Together we run a course centre and spend the income on community projects. We share responsibility for our home and the land on which we live. Most of us share a meal each evening and at least 15 birthdays a year (cake, candles and song). We participate in the wider community, promoting awareness of everyone's impact on the enviroment, through the local recycling scheme, community open days and the village com-

Year started 1983
Ideological focus ecological

Morchard Bishop,
Crediton, Devon EX17 6RF England
Telephone 01363 877228 **Fax** 01363 877587
Electronic Mail beechhill@ukonline.co.uk
World Wide Web http://web.onetel.net.uk/~beechhill

munity composting scheme. Some individuals earn their income in the wider world in journalism, education, recycling, complementary health, alternative ceremonies and training in Equal Opportunities; some work from home. We do not want our community to be a place of dogmatism, judgement or preaching. We value our diversity and flexibility. We aim to care for one another and enjoy life as it happens. We welcome each others' differences and enjoy visitors and volunteers - please send an SAE.

BHAKTIVEDANTA MANOR

•••••••••••••••••••••••••••••••

Bhaktivedanta Manor is the main centre of the International Society for
Krishna Consciousness in the UK. It is
67 acres of gardens, lake, woodland and
pastures. Over 100 single students of
Krishna consciousness study and serve at the
Manor with other families participating also
in daily services and activities (140 members
and their children live in the local area). The
spiritual focus is the worship of Radha-
Krishna in the traditional Vaishnava style. All
meals are lacto-vegetarian and the grounds
supply a lot of the flowers and vegetables
needed for the community. A herd of life-
time-protected cows and bulls provide the
milk and the muscle for hauling and plough-
ing on the site. The Manor is open for new
members, but all devotees living on the
property must be willing to comply with the
basic standards of the community - no

Year started 1973
Ideological focus worship of Krishna (Hindu)

Dharum Marg, Hilfield Lane, Aldenham
Watford , Hertfordshire WD25 8EZ England
Telephone 01923 857244 **Fax** 01923 852896
World Wide Web http://krishnatemple.com

meat-eating, no intoxication of any type
(including cigarettes, tea, coffee), no gam-
bling and no pre- or extra-marital sex. The
lifestyle of Krishna consciousness involves an
awakening of the realisation that we are not
these material bodies, we are the spirit soul
within, the eternal children of God whom
we know as Krishna. By chanting the holy
names of Krishna and serving to our best
capacity and devotion, we can uncover our
true spiritual personalities and discover the
pure love of God. We finally won our 15-
year campaign for
a new access
drive which
allows visi-
tors to
continue
attending
worship
and
classes.

BIRCHWOOD HALL COMMUNITY

Birchwood Hall is a large 19th century red brick house near the Malvern Hills. Within our eight acres we have woodlands, large vegetable garden, orchard and lawns. A converted Coach House is home to an additional six co-op members. There is also a small residential centre called "Anybody's Barn", a registered charity. The community currently comprises nine adults and one child. We have room for more and think the group would be enhanced by the addition of more children (and their parents). Most community members have some form of paid employment. Current occupations include: Architect, Photographer, Teacher, Sports administrator, GP, Artist and Clinical Psychologist. A focal point of community life is our daily shared evening meal. We also have weekly meetings where we discuss practical and

Year started 1970
Ideological focus none

Birchwood Hall, Storridge,
Malvern, Worcestershire WR13 5EZ England
Electronic Mail paddymcc@netcomuk.co.uk

business issues, exchange ideas and even sometimes try and have fun!

Everyone pays a weekly rent, adjusted to reflect income and circumstances. Rents include contributions to a fund we call "Other than Ourselves", which we allocate annually to charities and causes.

We live communally because this meets many of our personal and political needs and beliefs. We do not try to be self-sufficient although a number of us enjoy growing organic vegetables. We have a broad sympathy for many green ideas and causes and we try to lead an ecologically responsible lifestyle.

BLACKCURRENT HOUSING CO-OP

Blackcurrent is a housing co-operative and resource centre situated in an old school near the centre of Northampton. We are in the process of renovating this run-down building and using it as a show house for environmentally friendly restoration of a Victorian building. The resource centre provides meeting space, library, exhibitions, workshops, juggling club, youth club, organic veg boxes and a weekly film show. Some people work full-time outside of the community; others work part-time and volunteer as much time as they choose to the running of the centre and the renovation work.

All communal food is vegan and organic, and the house is a meat/fish/poultry/egg-free zone. We don't keep pets or livestock. We heat the house with woodstoves run on salvaged wood. We have a garden where we

Year started 1988
Ideological focus nonviolence

24 St Michael's Avenue,
Northampton, NN1 4JQ England
Telephone 0845 458 8259
Electronic Mail blackcurrent@lineone.net
World Wide Web http://anarres.info

grow some of our own food, veganically.
Toxic chemicals are not allowed in the
house or garden.
We have no com-
munal TV or radio,
preferring to make
our own music, play
table tennis, dance
and juggle.
We welcome visitors
who would like to
work with us, and
charge £3 a day for
food and a room.
Ring or email before
coming for our visi-
tor information
sheet.

BRAMBLES
HOUSING CO-OP

Brambles is a home for an eclectic mix of people and urban wildlife and a stop-over point for many more. We come from a mix of genders and social backgrounds with a wide range of skills to share and between us explore and promote co-operative ways of living.

The co-op itself has been running for over 10 years and has housed over 40 people during this time with members staying from months to many years.

We share two neighbouring houses, vegetable patches, fruit trees, wildlife garden and frog pond in a vibrant multicultural but economically poor area of Sheffield. Brambles provides its members with a secure, supportive environment from which we both work together and do our own stuff too.

Year started 1992
Ideological focus anarchist and ecological

80-82 Andover Street, Pitsmoor,
Sheffield, South Yorkshire S3 9EH England

The co-op acts as a focal point for resources
and information and as a free meeting space
for local groups.

We are working on plans to open as a
resource centre and radical library for use
by the local community.

Brambles is ecological and anarchic in focus
with no rotas and very few, but fair bound-
aries and a lot of learning under our collective belts.

Solar water heating is being installed, communal meals generally happen and the recycling and compost systems are pretty funky
and efficient.

BRAZIERS
ADULT COLLEGE

Founded in 1950, Braziers is a non-religious community and a college. The main house is Strawberry Hill Gothic in style and is set in 50 acres of unspoilt Oxfordshire countryside. Around a dozen long-term residents with a variety of backgrounds and interests live here and, in addition, there are usually five or six foreign students who come to improve their English and help run the College. Braziers is broadly evolutionist in outlook and has a particular interest in group process and group communication. We run our own educational programme - mainly at weekends - but we are also available as a venue for outside groups. Visitors may either stay in the house or opt to camp in the meadows. There are 22 bedspaces in the house, but camping allows us to accommodate much larger groups. The cooking has a vegetarian emphasis, but

Year started 1950
Ideological focus evolutionist ecological

Braziers Park, Ipsden,
Wallingford, Oxfordshire OX10 6AN England
Telephone 01491 680221 **Fax** 01491 680221
Electronic Mail admin@braziers.org.uk
World Wide Web http://www.braziers.org.uk

meat dishes are also served. Many of the vegetables come from our own organic kitchen garden. One of our newest ventures involves Permaculture. We are working closely with the Permaculture Academy with the intention of running permaculture courses at Braziers and increasing the sustainable output of the land. Low cost work weekends will soon be available for anyone who wants to come and help us with this experiment. The atmosphere at Braziers is informal, relaxed and supportive. Many people come here simply for a break or to complete a personal work project in tranquility. We would like to encourage this. If you would like to know more about Braziers, would like to receive our course brochure or want to find out about hiring Braziers as a venue, please ring us.

BRITHDIR MAWR

As stewards of this 165-acre farm, we try to live our lives working with rather than against nature, husbanding goats, cows, ducks, chickens and bees for milk, eggs and honey, keeping horses for carting and haymaking, and producing organic fruit and vegetables from polytunnels and large gardens. We coppice wood for fuel, bake bread, preserve produce, and use our own materials, such as wood and willow, for craftwork.

Accommodation is the traditional-built farmhouse and its outbuildings, electricity is supplied by wind, water and solar, toilets are composting, and we have a number of green design buildings.

Communal activities include 2-3 meals/week (vegetarian) and 1-2 workdays/week.

We run occasional courses and camps, and

Year started 1994
Ideological focus sustainable

Ffordd Cilgwyn,
Trefdraeth, Sir Benfro SA42 0QJ Wales
Telephone 01239 820164
Electronic Mail brithdir@brithdirmawr.freeserve.co.uk
World Wide Web http://www.brithdirmawr.com

are able to host small gatherings and workshops.

Visitors are very welcome, either self-cater-
ing in our hostel for £7/night (£3.50 children) or involved more directly with the
community itself at no monetary cost, in
exchange for 4 hours work a day, on a short
or longer term basis.

Languages spoken are Welsh, English,
Dutch, French, Spanish and Italian. Smoking
is restricted to private living spaces, and outside. We are currently actively seeking
new members.

BROTHERHOOD CHURCH

• •

The Brotherhood Church is a Christian Pacifist Group and has been in existence for over 100 years. Around 1892 it was jointly at Purley in Essex with Tolstoyans.

In 1898 the Tolstoyans in the group decided to move to Whiteway near Stroud in Gloustershire. The rest of the group, Christian Pacifists, moved to Yorkshire, moving around a bit, but mainly in Yorkshire, in the Leeds area. This group was very strong in its opposition to the government during WWI.

Quite a number of the men spent two and a half years in prison for not fighting, others, both men and women went to prison for writing and distributing anti-war leaflets. This tradition continues to the present day.

Year started 1921
Ideological focus christian/pacifist/ecological

Stapleton,
Pontefract, Yorkshire WF8 3DF England
Telephone 01977 620381

Around 1920 members felt the need to have contact with Mother Earth, a seven and a half acre field was bought and bungalows built without any resort to planning permission.
This land is probably some of the oldest organic holdings in Britain. Our Members and Trustees do not all live here at Stapleton but give their support from all corners of Britain.
We live out an ecological lifestyle, some refer to us as Anarchist, but it is really a Christian Pacifist lifestyle.
We have a large Strawberry Tea Gathering in early July and usually a smaller evening event in October. Visitors are welcome at all times.

BRYNDERWEN VEGAN COMMUNITY

B rynderwen (Welsh for oak tree hill) is a spacious four-bedroom house on the outskirts of Swansea, lying a short journey from the beautiful Gower coastline. A huge double garage could be converted to further accommodation, or to a work-shop, or both. There's a terraced garden, and an acre or two of adjoining land is being purchased - to be developed as a tree and shrub nursery, and for growing food vegan-organically.

Our views on life are diverse, with veganism as a common bond. We recognise that veg-anism can be approached from many differ-ent directions, and that some tolerance is needed. Even so conversation can be lively! We're involved with local vegan/vegetarian groups, and we run the Vegan Summer

Year started 2002
Ideological focus vegan

Brynderwen, Crymlyn Road, Llansamlet
Swansea, SA7 9XT Wales
Telephone 01792 792442
Electronic Mail vegancom@btinternet.com
WWW http://www.veganviews.org.uk/brynderwen

Gathering (a one week national event).
The aim over the next few years is to
expand and to attract others (with or without capital, and of any age), either joining us
in our projects or developing their own.
These might be of a social, business or educational nature. Some people may live at
Brynderwen, some at a possible second
property, and others may prefer to live inde-
pendently nearby. If you're interested in visiting, or knowing more, please contact us
for a newsletter.

BURTON BRADSTOCK OTHONA COMMUNITY

Othona invites you to live for a short while as part of a friendly, accepting community. Othona sees itself as 'rooted in the Christian heritage; open to a wider future'. In approaching spirituality we are light hearted, down to earth and unafraid to face change. Othona particularly suits people on or beyond the margins of church life and those struggling with the evolution of Christian faith. We affirm diversity among people in faith, spirituality, age, ability, race, background and sexual orientation.

For a new generation of retreat seekers we offer an informal community atmosphere, a simple lifestyle, and home cooking against a backdrop of great natural beauty. We schedule plenty of Open Space periods;

Year started 1946
Ideological focus christian/spiritual

Coast Road, Burton Bradstock,
Bridport, Dorset DT6 4RN England
Telephone 01308 897130 **Fax** 01308 898 205
Electronic Mail mail@othona-bb.org.uk
World Wide Web http://www.othona-bb.org.uk

time for personal retreat in a community
setting, often with a creative arts option.
Othona is distinguished by the way visitors
can join in a whole rhythm of life, from gardening to leading chapel services. Singing,
music, silence, candles, meditation are part
of our life. Events during the school holidays are usually child friendly.

Our stone house in 6 acres on the West
Dorset coast
can accommo-
date 30 visi-
tors. Walking
on famous
Chesil beach,
bird-watching
and rambling
are popular
here.

CAMPHILL RUDOLF STEINER SCHOOLS

The Camphill-Rudolf Steiner-Schools, which are situated on three estates in Royal Deeside, provide curative education for children with special needs ranging in age from 5 to 19.

A total of 150 co-workers live together with 118 pupils in 20 family units: the co-workers share the work that has to be done - teaching, caring, household tasks, gardening, etc. In the traditional Camphill household the child is part of a 'family' unit, which approximates closely to what one might term a 'normal' family environment where there is continuity and consistency of treatment, organisational stability and a sense of personal security. From the foundation of the first Camphill community by Dr Karl König, it has been recognised that all children have strengths and weaknesses and that it is the

Year started 1940
Ideological focus anthroposophy

Central Office, Murtle House, Bieldside
Aberdeen, AB15 9EP Scotland
Telephone 01224 867935 **Fax** 01224 868420
Electronic Mail b.porter@crss.org.uk
World Wide Web http://www.camphillschools.org.uk

responsibility of those working in Camphill
settings to develop the assets that each child
possesses. To that end, an holistic approach
is taken to the individual's physical, psycho-
logical, social and spiritual needs.
At a time when there is general disquiet at
the spiritual bleakness of living in a society
preoccupied with short-term and materialis-
tic concerns, Camphill communities make
no apology for their celebration of Christian
Festivals, their dedication to Christian values
and translating those values into action.

CANON FROME COURT

The main house and stable block contain 18 leasehold self-contained living spaces of varying sizes, housing some 26 adults, (32-69) and seventeen children (0-17).

We also have a meeting room for our weekly meetings (decisions by consensus); communal guest rooms; a dairy kitchen for making cheese, yoghurt and butter; a communal dining room for shared meals on Saturdays, holidays and other occasions and where we also host workshops (basket making, yoga, herbal medicine); the gym which is a huge hall, for parties, ceilidhs and singing and dance workshops; and a shop for wholefoods and chocolate.

There are also communal workspaces for metal and woodwork. Our mixed farm of 35 acres supports a variety of animals —

Year started 1978
Ideological focus ecological

Ledbury, Herefordshire HR8 2TD England
Telephone 0870 765 0711
Electronic Mail membership@canonfromecourt.org.uk
World Wide Web http://www.canonfromecourt.org.uk

dairy and beef cattle, goats, sheep, chickens, bees and Christmas geese. The huge walled garden produces year-round veg from year round work, with some help from WWOOFers. Then there is the front lawn for picnics, barbecues and the children's play area, a lake for boating and wild life and even a swimming pool. Canon Fromers like to work, rest and play!

CENTRE FOR ALTERNATIVE TECHNOLOGY

Our community is a constituent part of the Centre for Alternative Technology which promotes and implements renewable energy, ecological building, energy efficiency, sustainable sewage treatment, and organic growing. We twelve residents are all CAT volunteers or staff and their families. We live in either low-energy timber-framed homes or eco-renovated slate quarry worker's cottages. We are self-sufficient in drinking water filtration and reed bed sewage treatment. Our electricity is sourced from on-site wind, hydro and solar generation or "green electricity" import/export.

We have 4 communal meals a week, organise fire-wood, organic food & laundry collectively to save money, reduce our environmental impact and learn from each other. On recent community work days we

Year started 1975
Ideological focus pragmatic

CAT Community, Llwyngwern Quarry,
Machynlleth, Powys SY20 9AZ Wales
Telephone 01654 702400 **Fax** 01654 702782
Electronic Mail info@cat.org.uk
World Wide Web http://www.cat.org.uk

have built a compost loo, eco-renovated a
house, planted fruit trees and improved our
firewood sheds. Decision making is
achieved at regular com-
munity meetings
and is almost
entirely by
consensus.
The CAT
visitor centre
(excludes our
homes) is
open to day
visitors all
year round.
We also host
short-term and
long-term volunteers.
Applications for volunteer-
ships should be made by post or email with
CV to Rick Dance, since we have a waiting
list.

CLANABOGAN CAMPHILL COMMUNITY

••••••••••••••••••••••••••••••••••

Camphill Community Clanabogan lies on a property of 70 acres in the beautiful rolling countryside of Co Tyrone, four miles from the town of Omagh. About 70 people live in six households, some large, some small.

The community shares life and work with adults with learning disabilities. There are six family-style house communities. Workshops include a bakery, weavery and woodworkshop. A large biodynamic farm provides milk and meat and there are fresh vegetables from the garden.

A holistic life is built up with educational and cultural activities, social events and interaction with the locality. The community is Christian based, but the individual can make a free choice about participation.

Year started 1984
Ideological focus anthroposophical

15 Drudgeon Road, Clanabogan, Omagh, County Tyrone
BT78 1TJ Northern Ireland
Telephone 028 82256100 **Fax** 028 82256114
Electronic Mail camphill@btconnect.com

Part of the international camphill movement
founded on Rudolf Steiner's anthroposophy.

THE COMMUNITY PROJECT

•••••••••••••••••••••••••••••••••••••••

We are a large co-housing group living in a converted hospital with 24 acres of land. We have a training room with conference facilities for hire. On Friday evenings we share a potluck dinner, and here is a description of how it feels to cook for other people:
When I first cooked for the whole group I was petrified that my humble offering would not be up to scratch. Having only cooked for me and my hungry family, I was not used to having my slops scrutinised. Therefore I was over-ambitious and went for stuffed marrow!
This dish was awkward to transport to our Community Building, and it went some of the way in the passenger seat of my car, encased in a smart foil coat. Yet it still managed to get squashed!
On arrival I spruced up my sad looking mar-

Year started 1998
Ideological focus none

care of Diggers & Dreamers
Telephone 01323 815724 **Fax** 01323 815702
Electronic Mail newmembers@laughtonlodge.org

row and tried to hide it behind something else. Throughout the meal I found myself monitoring who had braved hunking a portion of marrow, and how much they ate! I was completely stressed and unable to enjoy the meal, especially as lots of marrow remained untouched!

So my advice is: keep it simple, stick to vegetables and cheese and don't worry if nobody eats what you bring! A metaphor for community life!

CORANI HOUSING AND LAND CO-OP

Four adults and one young person live together in adjoining Corani houses in Leicester. We would like two more members to share with us this generous terraced housing, including two workshops and cellars. Three other members, not currently housed by Corani, live elsewhere in Leicester. We are open to different needs and different backgrounds. We welcome, by arrangement, visitors who will help out and/or participate whilst with us.

The members living together aim to eat together most evenings and a self-determined rota decides who cooks. Corani owns one allotment and rents two others. One is being transformed into a forest garden supplying fruit, the others provide organically grown vegetables. Members are expected to income share. Capital is not essential but those that have capital are asked to deposit

Year started 1978
Ideological focus co-operative/sharing

12 Bartholomew Street,
Leicester, LE2 1FA England
Telephone 0116 254 5436 **Fax** 0116 255 5727
Electronic Mail info@corani.org

some with Corani. We have been known to
accept someone and their house!
Decision making is essentially pragmatic; by
consensus where all are concerned, otherwise with sensitive autonomy.
Things some or all of us like to do are: walking, gardening, growing vegetables, drama
club, woodcraft folk, dancing, watching
films, teaching, plumbing, carpentry, pho-
tography, collecting fruit stickers, slot car
racing, bird watching, promoting devolved
government, participating in a residents'
association, promoting sustainability, peer
counselling.

CORNERSTONE HOUSING CO-OPERATIVE

ornerstone is not so much a community as a collective of people who share the running of a housing co-op, but who have different political perspectives and focuses for their daily lives. Cornerstone consists of two large Victorian houses in Chapeltown, an ethnically diverse area of Leeds. Both houses need constant maintenance and have large gardens front and back where co-op members do their best to create beautiful and productive landscapes. Each house has space for seven members and there are short and long-term visitors swelling our numbers. A reasonably high turnover of members and visitors means new ideas and energy but also a pretty hectic atmosphere at times. Number 16 currently houses a cat and Number 40 houses a cat and a companion rat! Both houses have office space and computer

Year started 1993
Ideological focus multiple/diverse

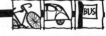

16 Sholebroke Avenue, Chapeltown,
Leeds, West Yorkshire LS3 3HB England
Telephone 0113 262 9365
Electronic Mail cornerstone@ukf.net
World Wide Web http://www.cornerstone.ukf.net

facilities. The broadly based aim of the co-
operative is that members are working for
social change and Cornerstone provides a
space where members pursue varied activities. These currently include two worker
co-ops (Footprint
printers co-op and
Viridian garden servic-
es), prisoner support,
animal rescue and
animal rights cam-
paigning, anti-militarist
campaigning,
indymedia support,
environmental direct
action, singing, dj-ing,
acting, temporary
social centre squatting
and supporting the
local community
amongst others!

COVENTRY PEACE HOUSE

Following a 13 month camp outside tank manufacturer Alvis, we bought six little houses in a row as a fully mutual housing co-op and permanent peace resource for Coventry and moved in on January 21st 1999. The houses are 15 minutes (walking) from the city centre, close to a canal and opposite a scrap yard and a Hindu temple. When the renovation is finished there will be a public peace and environmental library and a large meeting space (covering the ground floor of two houses) plus co-op living space. We run a project here working with local young people not in school, training or work and they are helping with the building. There will be disabled access to all of the ground floor, plus solar panels, grey water systems etc. We also do lots of work with refugees and campaign on peace and environmental issues including

Year started 1999
Ideological focus peace

311 Stoney Stanton Road,
Coventry, West Midlands CV6 5DS England
Telephone 024 7666 3031
Electronic Mail covpeace@gn.apc.org

the arms trade, sanctions against Iraq and
genetic engineering. We work closely with
the local community in many ways including running courses, peace education in
schools, neighbour mediation and our own
paid work. We have a large back garden
and an allotment nearby.

We are open to new members who must be
committed to non-violence and working
actively towards peace.

CRABAPPLE COMMUNITY

Crabapple's home is a slightly eccentric, crumbling Georgian house surrounded by 20 acres of beautiful woodland, pasture, orchards and vegetable, herb and flower gardens with heaps of potential and masses of thistles. All of us who live here have a deep enjoyment and love of the natural world and aspire communally to live in harmony with nature, treading as lightly on the earth as we sensibly can. Alongside our stewardship of the land we also aspire to create a safe, accessible, comfortable and happy environment in which people of all ages can grow as well as simply 'be'.

At present we're evolving suitable immediate, medium and long-term plans to take Crabapple forward with a more sustainable focus, one which, hopefully, will also involve us more in the wider community locally and

Year started 1975
Ideological focus non-ideological

Berrington Hall, Berrington,
Shrewsbury, Shropshire SY5 6HA England
Telephone 01743 761418

●●●●●●●●●●●●●●●●●●●●●●●●●●●●●●

globally, as well as preserving and carrying
the best of the community's past into the
future with us. Please write telling us a bit
about yourself if you would like to visit.

CREATING WELHEALTH CO-OPERATIVE

This is for people who are not yet fully committed to be full-time members of Welhealth (p 217), and who wish to work/support to acheive an autonomous vegan organic self sustainable structure built on the co-operative principle out of the rat race - no need for money or exchange. Members of Creating Welhealth are entitled to come for a holiday or short break on Welhealth land for free, and join in with the farm life, as little or as much as they want to, growing and picking the fruit of the land; and in order that there should be no "them and us" situation, members become part of the community while there, like friends or family; members are responsible for them-selves and hence share responsibility with all the others at the land. Pets are unwel-come, in order to encourage friendly wildlife, and the land is 100% vegan, so

Year started 1997
Ideological focus holiday vegan diggers

members who are not yet vegan are asked
to be vegan on Welhealth land.
The only people who can live on Welhealth
land are those who have been admitted
through an admission process and who
conform to the Welhealth constitution.

DARVELL BRUDERHOF COMMUNITY

●●●●●●●●●●●●●●●●●●●●●●●●●●●●●●●●

The Bruderhof is a movement of over 2,500 single adults, families and older people living in eleven communities in the UK, Germany, USA and Australia. Our two English communities are: Darvell Bruderhof, in Robertsbridge, East Sussex and Beech Grove Bruderhof in Nonington, Kent. Voluntarily pooling money, talents and energy, we base our life on the revolutionary vision and teaching of Jesus: Love each other and your enemies. Make peace. Don't judge. Don't worry about tomorrow. We try to connect with people the world over who struggle for justice, community and the value of all life. Our children are our primary concern. Babies are cared for at the community nursery while parents work; children attend Bruderhof schools. Our Plough Publishing House and our website serve as tools of dialogue. To put bread on our table

Year started 1920
Ideological focus christian

Robertsbridge, East Sussex TN32 5DR England
Telephone 01580 883300 **Fax** 01580 883317
Electronic Mail info@bruderhof.com
World Wide Web http://www.bruderhof.org.uk

we manufacture classroom equipment and
furniture, and aids for physically disabled
people. But our work is more than a business venture: from washing laundry to
assembling wooden products, work is 'love
made visible'. Visitors are welcome, but are
expected to join in communal activities and
work. Please write to arrange your stay, so
that we can work out accommodation
details.

EARTH HEART

Co-housing in rural Derbyshire with 8 homes, owned on 999 year leases, in a farmhouse and barn conversion (designed by a fantastic architect - ring for details!) with 20 acres of secluded woodland, river, and meadows, managed organically. Communal rooms, workshops and offices need converting. We are as ecological as we can manage/afford. Families here are committed to continuum style parenting, eg breast-feeding, family bed. Most children are home-educated, in an autonomous style, some choose school. We have community work days or weekends and 'sharing gatherings' once a month; business meetings twice a month (decisions by consensus); birthday parties regularly! Conflict resolution (often one-to-one) involves creative, active listening, sharing and 'owning' our part of any conflict

Year started 1998
Ideological focus child-centred

dynamic. People are very accepting and have mutually supportive, close friendships, working to achieve a good balance between individual/family privacy and social community life - which is stimulating, rich, challenging and rewarding.

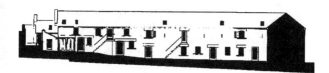

EARTHWORM HOUSING CO-OP

* *

Half-renovated, Edwardian house of character in 7 acres. Big farmhouse kitchen, gas cooker, wood/coal fired range, woodburners, library for all ages, tv room, music room ,tools, catering equipment, barns, polytunnels, greenhouse, renovated conservatory, party/play room, bikes, toys, tractor, noise. Cheeky children, wwoofers, visitors, rebellious pets. Stock-free farming, permaculture, veg garden, fruit, fat pheasants, birds, bats, toads, newts and worms. Compost loos, indoor loos, ponds, small wood, orchard, willow, weeds, outdoor fires.
Endless diy. Gardening, hurdlemaking, growing food. Scrabble, punk rock, hippies, music of the world. ART. Meetings, budgets

Year started 1989
Ideological focus ecological

accounts/letters, the ever-ringing phone.
Homebrew, salads, sosmix, and homegrown
spuds with tinned baked beans. (Often, not
always, communal meals). Shopping, tea
pots, the ever-boiling kettle.

Big old trees, the milky way, the moon all
year, good sunsets, village with school, pubs,
shops and swimmable river. More tea, fags
in the feng shui shed, thorny hands, nettle
stings, bad backs and poetry, ideas, debate.
A snapshot of the things we share.

We are joined by the land and our need to
look after and work it (in a cruelty-free and
organic way). Our desire for a better life,
and our willingness to share to get it. Our
rambly old house and the shelter and safety
it gives us.

This is WHEATSTONE/EARTHWORM in
2003. Please WRITE with an SAE BEFORE
visiting us...

EQUINOX HOUSING CO-OP

●●●●●●●●●●●●●●●●●●●●●●●●●●●●●●●●

Equinox Housing Co-op was set up in 1994 and moved into a large house in inner-city Manchester. Its aims were to provide affordable, quality accommodation to people involved in social change work. We are a group of 8 (plus dog) living communally and trying to build a supportive community based on the principles which we believe will help to make a better world. Our members are involved in a wide range of activities and projects including local community groups, non-violent direct action groups on many issues, ecological renovation, Manchester Environmental Resource Centre, herbalism, websites, woodlands, Radical Routes and many others. We also find time to enjoy the gardens, be sporty, play music and have (we are told) legendary parties. We have carried out extensive environmental improvements

Year started 1994
Ideological focus ecological

161 Hamilton Road, Longsight,
Manchester, M13 0PQ England
Telephone 0161 248 9224 **Fax** 0161 224 4648
Electronic Mail mail@eqnx.co.uk
World Wide Web http://www.eqnx.co.uk

(rainwater toilets, insulation, community office), and are looking towards further renovations (solar heating/PV, turf roof) which will make us more sustainable. The latest development is the opportunity to buy the derelict plot next door and do a radical inner-city-permaculture-self-build- eco-house-community-workshops project. Exciting times ahead!! Visitors and helpers welcome. Membership waiting list in operation — contact us.

ISLE OF ERRAID COMMUNITY

L iving on a tiny jewel of an island set into an emerald sea, our small community flourishes as we experience a sense of synchronicity with each other, our animals and the elements around us.

The heart of our community centres around our gardens as here we work hand-in-hand with nature to produce fruit and vegetables for our kitchen.

Accommodation is in our very cosy stone-built cottages heated by log burning stoves. Although primarily vegetarian, our kitchen also offers meat supplied by our animals. Our membership is quite small, only eight adults and one child, but there is always something going on, be it walks, boat trips, singalongs etc.

Year started 1977
Ideological focus sustainable-spiritual

Findhorn Foundation - Isle of Erraid, Fionnphort,
Isle Of Mull, Argyll PA66 6BN Scotland
Telephone 01681 700384
Electronic Mail bookings@erraid.fslife.co.uk
World Wide Web http://www.erraid.com

Our island community also opens its doors
to guests who stay with us anything ranging
from one week to a couple of years.
Meditation and singing play a part in our
lives as we meet daily to pursue both.
For further information, please contact us.

FASLANE PEACE CAMP

F aslane Peace Camp was set up in 1982 as a permanent and visible base for protest against the Faslane Naval Base. We live as a community, aiming to promote an alternative, more sustainable way of living based on nonviolence and cooperation. We welcome visitors at any time - let us know in advance if you can, but it's not essential. We live in caravans, benders and a treehouse. We each donate £12.50/week or £2/day (less for kids) for food and other expenses. All communal food is veggie/vegan. Dogs and children are welcome, but be aware that we are next to a busy road. Our focuses are: peace, nonviolence, direct action, nuclear disarmament, sustainability and community building. If you want to contact us, phoning is more reliable than emailing.

Year started 1982
Ideological focus peace, nonviolence

A814, Shandon,
Nr Helensburgh, Dumbartonshire G84 8NT
Telephone 01436 820901
Electronic Mail faslanepeacecamp@conscious.every1.net
World Wide Web www.faslanepeacecamp.org.uk

FINDHORN FOUNDATION

The only thing that stays the same at Findhorn, is change. People come here and experience inner changes: their hearts opening, their minds relaxing, their consciousness expanding. The community itself is always changing too: new management structures, new decision-making procedures, new initiatives moving forward - all the better to reflect the deeper issues and possible solutions of our times. After 40 years Findhorn is still committed to serving spirit, with "work is love in action" still being the most widely practised mode of service; it's just that the kinds of work keep changing and developing over the years. Where once the Findhorn Foundation was known as the place where people talked to nature spirits and grew 40-pound cabbages, it is now known for its community, its educational activities, and its develop-

Year started 1962
Ideological focus celebrating the divinity in all life

The Park, Findhorn,
Forres, Morayshire IV36 3TZ Scotland
Telephone 01309 690311 **Fax** 01309 690301
Electronic Mail enquiries@findhorn.org
World Wide Web http://www.findhorn.org

ing ecovillage (and some of us still do communicate directly with nature). All of these activities are the natural continuation of earlier work done in these areas. People from all over the world come to Findhorn for Experience Weeks and other courses, and many find inspiration to bring spirit more present in their everyday lives. The Findhorn Foundation is now the cornerstone of a wider community of almost 400 people, including 33 businesses, working together to create a sustainable lifestyle that reflects the divinity in all life.

FIRESIDE HOUSING CO-OP

Fireside is situated in the inner city of Sheffield. We are very lucky to live in an area where there is plenty of green space, our four adjacent terraced houses back onto a lovely old cemetery and there's an adventure playground at the end of the road. We share a large garden, in which there is plenty of space for the children from the co-op and their friends to play, space to grow our organic veg and ample space for fires and parties too. We have a wind generator and a solar panel which we use as a display at local festivals. We are interested in renewable energies on a national scale as well as small design projects at home. Each house is run as a separate household, so we have a lot of personal space. We do however eat communally on a regular basis, particularly when having a workday on the houses or gardens.

Year started 1996

61 Melrose Road,
Sheffield, South Yorkshire S3 9DN England
Telephone 0114 2781350
Electronic Mail fireside@blueyonder.co.uk

FOX HOUSING CO-OP

W e live as a community on a 70 acre farm. All are involved in our large box scheme which has organic produce from our 20 acres of field-scale crops, polytunnels and agro-forestry. The box scheme supports Welsh growers, offers alternatives to supermarkets, provides ethical income for us and local folk too. All profits are used to promote organics in our locality.

That's what we do — why we do it is because we want to take responsibility for ourselves in as many ways as possible. Providing good fresh food for others means that we eat well whilst reducing travel to work, food miles for the produce, bypass supermarkets etc. Others things we do to fulfil this aim are: vegan diet; personal growth supporting freedom from addiction; seeking spirituality in the land around us;

Year started 1998
Ideological focus ecological

Werndolau, Gelli Aur,
Carmarthen, Dyfed SA32 8NE Wales
Telephone 01558 668798 **Fax** 01558 668088
Electronic Mail roger@werndolau.fsnet.co.uk

home-educating our kids; consuming light-
ly/ethically; learning to be inter-dependant
etc.
We work hard, like clear structure/commu-
nication and 'do' our values rather than talk
about them (though we do sometimes!). We
eat/ play together, having 'community weekends' for quality time and fun.
We welcome visitors who help out and may
have paid opportunities to live/work here.
Enthusiasm for all things wholesome and
organic helps! Drop us a line if you're interested...

FRANKLEIGH HOUSE

Frankleigh Co-Flats consists of 6 self-contained flats converted from a grade 2 listed Victorian Mansion. There are shared grounds of about 7 acres, including an open air swimming pool, rose garden, front lawn, beech tree field and a large field to the south.

There is plenty of land in the south field for you to carve out an allotment. You will use the land under licence from the Management Company. The main condition will be that it must be gardened organically.

Year started 1995
Ideological focus cohousing

Bath Road,
Bradford-on-Avon, Wiltshire BA15 2PB England
Electronic Mail info@frankleigh.com
World Wide Web http://www.frankleigh.com

GAUNTS HOUSE
COMMUNITY

T he community at Gaunts House is informal and more inevitable rather than intentional. We are dedicated to profound learning, and to providing a peaceful, inspiring environment for others. Our structure includes members, guests, students, trainees, volunteers and employed staff. Our purpose is to seek, find and follow our individually right paths, and to provide care and support for others.

The work in our community consists of running every aspect of a country house, from the organic garden to housekeeping, as a venue for residential courses of a creative, healing, and spiritual nature. Basic jobs such as washing up are allocated by weekly rota, while larger and more diverse projects are taken up individually, or by group or department. While there is no defined doctrine here, a faith in the timeliness of all

Year started 1990

Wimborne, Dorset BH21 4JQ England
Telephone 01202 841522 **Fax** 01202 841959
Electronic Mail admin@rgf-gaunts.demon.co.uk
World Wide Web http://www.rgf-gaunts.demon.co.uk

things enables life to run fairly smoothly, if
sometimes a little chaotically. After all, with
Divine chaos, it's the divine that counts.
Regular meetings cover the day-to-day practicalities, while sharings and satsangs (profound discussions) allow us to enter into a
deeper mode of communication.
Meditation is encouraged, both individually
and collectively; as is spending time in the
beautiful grounds and countryside, com-
muning with nature. Life here is sometimes
intense, often challenging, and very rewarding. We welcome anyone to come see for
themselves, and we look forward to meeting
you.

GLYN ABBEY

We live in an old country estate of 10 acres. There are nine shares (the last share to change hands was 6 years ago). We have 9 separate households with 9 distinct dwellings, some still in the process of being 'reclaimed'. There are compost toilets, spring water, separate organic gardens (mainly), no management structure, no agreed ideology. Current age range is 9 to 60. The 17 adults include teachers, social workers, labourers, caterering staff, scientists, office and shop workers, horticulturalists, artists and artisans, writers, performers and musicians; some gainfully employed in the outside world and some not. Eight children are educated locally. Six 'ex-children' (over 18) return regularly from other parts. There are also two dogs, assorted cats and a few chickens.

Year started 1976
Ideological focus ecological

care of Diggers & Dreamers

We come together officially twice per year, at New Year and for our Mayfair, everything else is ad hoc. Some of us would like to learn how to structure meetings or community business in such a way that conflict or fear of conflict would not sabotage them; as we have no business meetings and no structure for such. Some of us would also like to offer places for WOOFERS and WOROODS (workers on restoration of old derelicts)!

GRIMSTONE COMMUNITY

Grimstone Manor is set in 27 acres of garden, pasture and wilderness on the edge of Dartmoor. The Community's main focus is to create and maintain a supportive space for a range of personal development groups who visit us throughout the year. We try to run our business with integrity, balancing its needs with those of the group participants, ourselves and the environment. We meet weekly, making decisions by consensus. Members share the core work as well as specialising in areas of particular interest. Work is paid at a common hourly rate. Our future is a continual topic for discussion and we are open to new developments regarding the Community itself and the groups that we welcome here. In the past two years individual Community Members have developed projects as varied as a local

Year started 1990
Ideological focus eco-spiritual

community composting scheme, an eco-psy-chology network, a local com-munity choir, and a monthly acoustic music cafe raising money for local chari-ties in Tavistock. We are open to enquiries from long- and short-term volunteers, woofers and possible new Members with energy, skills, (and in the case of the Members, capital) who are keen to join us in this caring, supportive and beautiful space to live and grow.

GWERIN HOUSING ASSOCIATION

· ·

Gwerin is a community of five houses, four of which are part of a Victorian terrace. These large houses are shared between members of the Association. Each house is run differently, according to the individuals who live there. We have weekly meetings where the whole membership comes together to discuss the running of the Association. We are a mixture of individuals, and as a community have no particular ideological focus. Gwerin now holds five properties. We operate on a small budget produced by rents, and the labour of all members in renovation of the properties and supporting the decisions of the weekly group meetings. Every aspect of the Association is open to scrutiny by all members who, in turn, volunteer their skills to ensure that the rules of the constitution are tempered by the day-to-day reality of

Year started 1977
Ideological focus consensual co-operative

121 Hagley Road, Old Swinford,
Stourbridge, West Midlands DY8 1RD England
Electronic Mail Gwerin@discordian.co.uk

life in the Community. Gwerin also strives to
support adults with special needs, in a
Community atmosphere, using our strong
ties with Dudley Social Services. The
Coachouse Project is now well established,
in partnership with St.Mary's Church, with
Gwerin members situated in the Cottage
overseeing a workshop at the Coachouse,
offering various arts/crafts activities at cost
to the local community.

HARGRAVE ROAD COMMUNITY

●●◆◆●●◆●●◆◆◆●◆◆●◆●◆◆●◆◆◆◆◆◆●◆◆●

High fibre compost and lots of apples, Joanna's great gourds, green woodworking with Adrian or tea ceremony with Ashley. Tell a story to Caroline... do you have something to grow in John's green house? Check out tales from the past with house historian Robert and eat David's kulfee, could you help Lilly and Maria?

All in a purpose-built communal house, once monthly meetings, shared communal duties and considerate living.

The raised beds have just been finished, next project, the earth oven... and so it goes on... want to get involved?

Year started 1987
Ideological focus ecological/care

4 Hargrave Road, Archway,
London, N19 5SJ England

HEARTWOOD COMMUNITY

We are a Housing Co-operative located on a 35-acre farm 6 miles south of Carmarthen. The land has 8 acres of beautiful oak and ash woodland with streams running through it, and 13 acres of good quality pasture and some unimproved land. We intend to plant trees on most of the land. We also want to create a Forest Garden and wildflower meadow as well as developing more areas for growing food.

There is currently a three-bedroom house with planning permission for an extension and some outbuildings, which we plan to convert using eco-friendly methods. Over time, we intend to create further individual and family units and large areas for community use — communal kitchen, bathrooms, lounge, utility and storage spaces, and workshops. We are a group of people who have a background in personal growth and work

Year started 1997
Ideological focus eco-spiritual

Blaen Y Wern, Llangyndeyrne,
Kidwelly, Sir Gaerfyrddin SA17 5ES Wales
Electronic Mail hippiesontour@yahoo.com

with people - counselling, mediation,
youthwork, management consultancy and
teaching. We have lived together since
1997, spending 2 years looking for our farm,
and have spent much time nurturing our
personal relationships. The core of our community rests on how we develop and sustain
our relationships and our practise of
Permaculture includes sustainable relationships with each other as well as with the
land we live on. We share rituals and life
events together in a way that is meaningful,
spiritual and respectful. We make plans with
the generations to come in mind. We share
incomes, car(s), meals, a washing machine
and lots of trust! We have created one new
'member' in the years we've been together,
who is now a toddler, and we are currently
looking for other people, who share our values, to join us. Please write or email if you
want to know any more about us and how
you might become a part of what we are
creating.

THE HIVE HOUSING CO-OP

Welcome are from a diverse range of tendencies (anarchist, socialist, suicidal...) united by a shared belief in social change through grassroots action [solidarity & eco campaigns, housing & human rights, community food growing & catering...] and of course, co-operation. We reached a limit of tolerance of squalid living conditions and naughty landlords that dominate the Bradford property scene. So we decided to own our own squalid living conditions, in a friendly, sustainable and DIY manner.

We joined the Radical Routes network of little fish, borrowed some money and bought a 4-storey Victorian terrace house in inner-city sunny Manningham in 1997. Since then we've been blundering along, fine-tuning

Year started 1997

c/o 17-21 Chapel St,
Bradford, West Yorkshire B15 DT England
Telephone 01274 745002
Electronic Mail the_hive_coop@yahoo.com

our DIY skills and creating a solid base for
our other activities. Amongst other things
we've been insulating, messing with slates,
and developing our backyard garden. Our
latest feature is a double bunk-bed so we
can do B&B for various punk bands and all
and sundry. And yes we're still trying to find
space to accommodate our bicycle breed-
ers.

We see the Hive as a demonstration of how
people's home life can be organised in a
more humane, ecological and fulfilling way,
and also as a catalyst for changing our society
into one that embodies these qualities. We
still dream of serious eco-renovation, a uni-
lateral declaration of independence, and a
permanently tidy hallway.

HOCKERTON HOUSING PROJECT

T he Hockerton Housing Project (HHP) is the UK's first earth sheltered, self-sufficient ecological housing development. The residents of the five houses generate their own clean energy, harvest their own water and recycle waste materials causing minimal pollution or carbon dioxide emissions. The houses are amongst the most energy efficient, purpose-built dwellings in Europe. The houses are the focus of a holistic way of living, which combines the production of organic foods, low intensity fish farming, promotion of wildlife, and the planting of thousands of trees.

The project was conceived in the early 1990s. It took two years to complete the planning agreement with the local authority and a further two years to build the homes and facilities.

Over the years the project has established itself as an exemplar of sustainable development. As a result of this it has developed a

Year started 1995
Ideological focus none

The Watershed, Gables Drive, Hockerton
Southwell, Nottinghamshire NG25 0QU England
Telephone 01636 816902
Electronic Mail hhp@hockerton.demon.co.uk
World Wide Web http://www.hockerton.demon.co.uk

range of services through the creation of a small on-site business. This workers' co-operative provides a level of employment for its members, whilst promoting sustainable development. Its activities include running guided tours, workshops, talks, consultancy and, soon to be launched, a match-making service.

Although each family has their own home, the community share food growing, site maintenance, managing the facilities and a common sustainable business.

HOLY ROOD HOUSE

A place of peace and tranquillity, overlooking the Hambledon Hills, the Centre for Health and Pastoral Care offers therapeutic and safe space for people of all ages.

Discovering acceptance and a relaxed environment, guests find empowerment to work towards their own health and well-being, with professional support from counsellors, psychotherapists, masseurs and creative arts therapists. The friendship and care of staff and the residential community, excellent home-cooking, gardens and animals, laughter and sharing, create a sense of belonging, and a few days or a couple of weeks becomes an important oasis in life for many people.

The gentle Christian ethos of this open, radical community, offers a space for guests to develop their own journey in a way that is

Year started 1993
Ideological focus christian

10 Sowerby Road, Sowerby,
Thirsk, North Yorkshire Y07 1HX England
Telephone 01845 522580
Electronic Mail holyroodhouse@centrethirsk.fsnet.co.uk
World Wide Web http://www.holyroodhouse.freeuk.com

right for them. Celebrating spiritual diversity,
the community reflects theologically through
research, accredited modular work and con-
ferences arranged through The Centre for
The Study of Theology and Health, an offshoot of Holy Rood House.
Whatever draws you to Holy Rood House,
as an individual or as a group, you will be
sure to find it a special place, and we can
be sure that our lives will be enriched by
your visit.

INVERNESS L'ARCHE COMMUNITY

L'Arche Inverness is part of the world-wide federation of L'Arche communities founded by Jean Vanier in 1964, that aims to build community with people with learning disabilities.

Our community is based in the capital of the Scottish Highlands and consists of households where community members share life together. Between 3 and 14 people live together, those with learning disabilities and those who come as 'assistants', sharing in every aspect of daily living; shopping, cooking, celebrating, going out and praying together. As a Christian community, our values are based on the Gospels, but we are happy to welcome those of other faith traditions.

Year started 1975
Ideological focus christian

Braerannoch, 13 Drummond Crescent,
Inverness, IV2 4QR Scotland
Telephone 01463 239615 **Fax** 01463 711089
Electronic Mail inverness@larche.org.uk
World Wide Web http://www.larche.org.uk/inverness

Assistants come from all over the world,
some for a minimum of one year, others to
make the Community their long-term home,
including those who have families and live
alongside community houses. We have
three workshops where we can offer a place
of meaningful work to community members, and we sell our woodwork, candles
and plants. We meet together regularly for
community events to enjoy moments of
laughter, or to share the deeper aspects of
our common humanity.
L'Arche involves a challenge to grow and
develop, to learn new skills and to experience all that community implies.

KEVERAL FARM COMMUNITY

•••••••••••••••••••••••••••••••••••

Keveral Farm has existed as a community in various forms since 1973. It consists of 15 adults, 8 children, 6 dogs, 5 cats, 6 chickens and a cackle of scrap vehicles.

The main house and farm buildings are owned and managed by our housing co-operative, One Community. We aim to reach decisions by consensus, but we also have a voting procedure if required.

The 30 acres of farm land are owned by our land co-op Keveral Sustainable Landholdings Ltd, and leased to Keveral Farmers Ltd, our workers co-op, which manages the farm. Courses, including a full permaculture design course held annually in August, are run by Keveral Permaculture Group.

The workers co-operative is centred around an organic vegetable box scheme which

Year started 1973

Looe, Cornwall PL13 1PA England
Telephone 01503 250215
Electronic Mail visit@keveral.org
World Wide Web http://www.keveral.org

sells 150 veg boxes a week. We also produce organic preserves, shitaki mushrooms
and liquid feed, as well as running a small
campsite in our orchard field.

The growth of our farming enterprises are
due in part to fairly stable (numerically) residents. We rarely accept new members.
With 8 children all eight or under, we seem
to have moved in to a child-rearing phase.
We accept Wwoofers and working visitors
by arrangement, usually for 5-7 days. Our
camping fees (at the time of going to print)
are £3 per adult (£4 in August), £1 per child
over 5yrs, and £2 per car per night. We
prefer enquiries by email. Further info on
our website.

LAMBETH L'ARCHE COMMUNITY

L'Arche Lambeth is an ecumenical Christian community where adults with learning disabilities and their assistants live and work together.

There are five community households in the West Norwood area of South London, where between seven and fourteen people share daily life. Craft workshops — weaving, gardening, stonework and candle-making — provide work for community members who have learning disabilities.

Assistants support people either in their home (one of the community households) or at work. Assistants come from all over the world, whenever possible for a minimum of one year; some have made the community their long-term home.

Year started 1977
Ideological focus christian

15 Norwood High Street,
London, SE27 9JU England
Telephone 020 8670 6714 **Fax** 020 8670 0818
Electronic Mail info.lambeth@larche.org.uk
World Wide Web http://www.larche.org.uk/lambeth

L'Arche seeks to reveal the particular gifts of
people with learning disabilities who belong
at the very heart of their communities and
who call others to share their lives. In a
divided world, L'Arche wants to be a sign of
hope. Its communities, founded on
covenant relationships between people of
differing intellectual capacity, social origin,
religion and culture, seek to be a sign of
unity, faithfulness and reconciliation (from
the Charter of L'Arche).
For further information on becoming an
assistant, please contact the Assistants'
Co-ordinator.

THE LAND OF ROOTS

For several years this group has been growing, evolving, expanding, shrinking, searching, researching and changing. It is now a stable group of five members with an additional supporters group and advisory group. We are currently hoping to buy 42 acres of woodland in County Durham.

We now have half of the money and we need to raise a little more before we go to the bank for the rest.

Once bought we intend to establish an educational facility, start a timber and woodcrafts business, grow mushrooms, keep bees, build low-impact structures, grow willow, fruit and vegetables, make chairs and charcoal etc. The project is focused on a

Year started 2001
Ideological focus permaculture

14 Railway Street, Langley Park,
Durham, Co. Durham DH7 9YS England
Telephone 0191 3735109

balance between business, community and personal development. We will be using permaculture design techniques.

The group currently consists of a permaculture designer, woodworker, willow sculptor, celebrant, researcher and many other skills beyond.

LAURIESTON HALL

Twenty-eight of us, aged one to seventy-one, with occasional long-suffering, long-staying visitors, live in this rambling pink pile built around a sixteenth century fortified tower house. We co-operatively manage 135 acres of surrounding woodland, pasture and marsh, including the small corner of a loch (swimming in the summer, skating in the winter.)

We live semi-communally, collecting and processing every week the couple of tons of timber needed to keep the wood-stoves going. We grow fruit and vegetables on a prodigious scale and allow the hens, pigs, cows and bees to keep us busy. We do most of our own maintenance and keep the hydro-electric plant going. We gossip, play volleyball and endlessly relate to each other.

Year started 1972
Ideological focus elusive

Laurieston,
Castle Douglas, Dumfries & Galloway DG7 2NB Scotland
Electronic Mail evi@lauriestonhall.demon.co.uk

Visitors come on Maintenance Weeks (usually April, July and September) to help us with maintenance, gardening, land work and domestics. We also offer a full programme of week long events: music, self-help, creative, lesbian and gay etc.
Please send an A4 sized SAE (44p) for the newsletter.

It would be wrong to say we have no ideological focus, but we haven't decided what it is yet. We trust in each other to take as much control, individually and co-operatively, over our lives as we can. We believe in compost, laughing, wellies and freedom. Oh and the inevitability of change.

LEE ABBEY ASTON HOUSEHOLD COMMUNITY

We are a small ecumenical Christian community of adults, part of the wider Lee Abbey Movement, committed to living and working in a multi-faith, multi-racial area. Our Victorian terraced house has four single and one double bedrooms, a community lounge, kitchen and bathroom all upstairs. Downstairs has facilities which can be used by others in the neighbourhood for committee meetings, quiet days etc, with a pleasant garden.

We meet together for prayer around the breakfast table, and eat our evening meal together, often with other 'friends of the community' joining us. We share the tasks of shopping, cleaning, cooking and entertaining, and pool our wages or benefits, receiving a weekly amount for personal use. We have a community car, but two of us

Year started 1988
Ideological focus christian

121 Albert Road, Aston,
Birmingham, West Midlands B6 5ND England
Telephone 0121 326 8280

cycle whenever possible. We try to reach
decisions by consensus, when we remember, and are committed to spending time
together, supporting, encouraging and listening to each other. We do paid or voluntary work, spend time with
local folk, offer hospitality,
and share our faith
as and when appro-
priate. Each of us is
an active member of
a local fellowship or
church, and we
want to deepen our
faith.

We offer a support-
ive, reflective,
prayerful environ-
ment in which to
experience life in the
inner city. Enquiries
welcome.

LIVERPOOL L'ARCHE COMMUNITY

L'Arche means 'the Ark' and began in France in 1964, when Jean Vanier said 'yes' to God's call to share his life with two men with learning disabilities. From this call grew an international federation of communities where people with learning disabilities and assistants share daily life through living, working and praying together, rediscovering the depth of the Gospel and the love of God for each one of us. The L'Arche Liverpool Community opened its first house in 1976. Four more community houses have since opened, along with a house of prayer and a flat for more independent supported living. A workshop, The Ark, is the focus for craft, horticultural and therapy projects and a work experience scheme with local employers. Older members enjoy activities geared towards a slower

Year started
Ideological focus Christian

The Ark , Lockerby Road,
Liverpool, L7 0HG England
Telephone 0151 260 0422 **Fax** 0151 263 2260
Electronic Mail liverpool@larche.org.uk
World Wide Web http://www.larche.org.uk/liverpool

pace of life, while a shop sells handicrafts. The community presently provides home and work to 23 people with learning disabilities, and a similar number of residential assistants (others work at The Ark), while The Ark also welcomes ten more people with learning disabilities who live locally.

We often have vacancies for assistants, mainly in the community houses. We normally ask applicants to make a commitment of a year.

LOCH ARTHUR CAMPHILL COMMUNITY

Loch Arthur Community lies 6 miles from Dumfries, by the village of Beeswing. At present we have over 500 acres of land, including farmland, a large loch and forested areas. We have established 5 households, the smallest of which has a house community of 9 people and the largest a house community of 19 people. There are 68 people in the community, including families with children, handicapped adults and other co-workers who join us for periods from a few weeks to several years.

Work activities in Loch Arthur include farming, gardening, estate work, creamery, bakery, weaving workshop and housework. We do not have hours 'on and off' duty, but we try to remain aware of each others need at all times. We attempt to live and work together in a way which recognises the

Year started 1984
Ideological focus anthroposophy

Beeswing,
Dumfries, DG2 8JQ Scotland
Telephone 01387 760687 **Fax** 01387 760618
Electronic Mail chanarin@btinternet.com

all times. We attempt to live and work together in a way which recognises the dignity and uniqueness of each human being and does not distinguish between those who are called handicapped and those who are not. We share an active cultural and social life.

No-one receives wages but all basic needs are met by the community and everyone receives an amount of pocket money. We welcome enquiries by letter and phone and are happy to arrange visits.

LOSANG DRAGPA
BUDDHIST CENTRE

Losang Dragpa Centre is a Buddhist college and meditation centre situated in the beautiful countryside of the West Yorkshire Pennines. We have an international community of about 30 people, both lay and ordained, male and female from all walks of life. Our vision, which lies at the heart of everything we do, is to help increase peace and happiness in the world. We aim to achieve this by making the timeless wisdom of Buddhism available to everyone in a way that is simple practical and effective. We believe everyone can find lasting happiness, peace and contentment and we teach people how to experience this through meditation and positive thinking. We run regular evening classes, day and weekend courses and retreats covering all

Year started 1985
Ideological focus buddhist

aspects of meditation and Buddhism attracting people from the local community, around the UK and from all over the world. Everyone, regardless of religion or background is welcome to sample life in a friendly Buddhist community on a working holiday, where you get delicious vegetarian meals and accommodation in exchange for 35 hours work per week. There are many opportunities to get involved in the busy life of this friendly community including office work, cooking, building maintenance, groundwork and gardening all in a beautiful and spiritual environment.

Please feel free to come and stay for an informal and relaxing break!

LOTHLORIEN COMMUNITY

Lothlorien is a therapeutic community for people with mental health problems. We have links with Samye Ling Tibetan Centre in Dumfriesshire. Buddhist values of compassion and tolerance are the basis of our approach, but we are not a religious community and we are open to everyone.

The community consists of 8 people with mental health problems and 4 voluntary co-workers, living in a large log house on 17 acres of land. The 3 staff, who provide a continuity of support to the community, are non-resident.

We have a strong belief in everyone's potential for well being, even in the midst of pain and distress. We believe that people need not be imprisonsed by their past. We aim to help people to develop their strengths and work towards recovery

Year started 1978
Ideological focus buddhist

Corsock,
Castle Douglas, Kirkcudbrightshire DG7 3DR Scotland
Telephone 01644 440602
Electronic Mail lothlorien1@btopenworld.com
World Wide Web http://www.lothlorien.tc

through the shared experience of community life. We avoid diagnosing or labelling and
attempt to break down the distinction
which frequently exists between those seen
as 'well' and those seen as 'unwell'.
The ordinary practical tasks of community
life, such as gardening, cooking and cleaning have a grounding effect and the rhythm
of daily life provides a structure which helps
to restore a sense of balance to people's
lives. Relaxation, artwork, massage and Tai
Chi are also part of the programme.
Central to the life of the community is the
daily meeting, where we plan work and
other activities, make decisions and attempt
to address issues of living together as a
group in an open way.
Lothlorien has vacancies on a regular basis,
as the maximum stay is two years. Please
contact the Project Manager for further
details.

MONIMAIL TOWER PROJECT

I n 1985 a community was started on the land around an ancient Tower. Most of the land is woodland. There is also a large orchard and walled garden. We live in a Segal self-build house and also in rooms in the Tower itself. Monimail Tower is the remains of Cardinal Beaton's Palace, built in the fifteenth century.

We are legally constituted as an educational charity promoting learning in the field of organic horticulture, and also aiming to benefit disadvantaged people. We run a diverse programme of courses and events and try to share as much as possible from food and work to skills and resources. We eat a mostly vegetarian diet, organic if possible. The main areas of responsibilty are the garden, the woods, building maintenance and

Year started 1984
Ideological focus ecological/sustainable

administration. We pay rent to the Project
and do not share income. We would like to
find more ways of becoming self supporting.
We also like to meet people, play music,
dance and generally have fun. We have
regular meetings and make our decisions by
consensus.

Our aim is to develop a resource for ourselves and other people with which to learn
how to live together in a way that is beneficial to all. We are open to people from
whatever background to visit and take part
and we host wwoofers who work for their
keep.

For more information on membership and
an up-to-date course programme please
write enclosing a stamped addressed enve-
lope or email us.

THE MONKEY SANCTUARY

• •

The Monkey Sanctuary has been a home to a colony of Amazonian woolly monkeys since 1964. It was established to provide a stable setting for woolly monkeys rescued from lives of isolation as pets and today the rescue work has extended to include other species of monkeys. A team of approximately 12 people work full-time, most of them live together in an old Victorian house on the premises. The core members are also assisted by volunteers who can spend anything between two weeks and several months at the Sanctuary. During the summer the sanctuary is open to the public and aside from caring for the monkeys, we spend most of our time with the visitors explaining the monkey's behaviours and telling them more about the dangers primates face both in the wild and in captivity. The winter months are dedicated

Year started 1964
Ideological focus ecological/animal welfare

Murrayton,
Looe, Cornwall PL13 1NZ England
Telephone 01503 262532 **Fax** 01503 262532
Electronic Mail info@monkeysanctuary.org
World Wide Web http://www.monkeysanctuary.org

to running educational programs in local schools, campaigning for the welfare and conservation of captive and wild monkeys and fund-raising for partner projects abroad.

Both our house and the monkey's territory are surrounded by a conservation garden designed to promote local plant species and wildlife and there is a strong emphasis on the ecological aspects of our community living. Having said that, the challenge of supporting a mixed community of monkeys and humans in an ecologically sustainable manner has yet to be fully met!

MONKTON WYLD COURT

Monkton Wyld Court is an educational charity run by a resident community of about a dozen adults, plus children and animals. The eleven acre grounds include a fifteen bedroom Victorian rectory, a converted stable block and other outbuildings, a large organic vegetable garden, terraced lawns, fields, woods and stream. Facilities include a library, meditation hut, art hut, pottery, workshop, healing room and piano room. Living at Monkton is a full-time commitment. Each morning, we meet together to talk and plan the day. Cooking, cleaning, milking the cows etc. is organised by rota, but each resident is also responsible for specific areas of work, from gardening to admin. We generate income through a programme of educational courses and other

Year started 1982
Ideological focus education/sustainability

events, and also run a kindergarten for the local community.

Our weekly community meetings alternate between "business" meetings where we make decisions by consensus, and "communication" meetings, where we address (inter) personal issues. We are committed to making continual improvements to our levels of ecological sustainability, and usefulness to the wider community as an educational resource.

We welcome volunteers to work with us for one week initially. Volunteers often return for longer visits, and sometimes end up living here.

MORNINGTON GROVE COMMUNITY

Without land, urban communities have a different rhythm to their rural counterparts, with much hive-like come-and-go at all hours as people depart and return for a wide variety of outside occupations. Somewhat the opposite of, perhaps, labouring together on a community-held smallholding. Mornington Grove is a city community of 14 diverse people of all ages, otherwise united by loosely libertarian, green, feminist and spiritual ideals. We live in the heart of London's densely-populated East End in a pair of imposing Victorian houses with a double garden. Mornington Grove began life as an offshoot of another London community, Some Friends. Last year — in some style — we celebrated our twentieth anniversary.

Year started 1982
Ideological focus indefinable

13 Mornington Grove, Bow,
London, E3 4NS England

We organise ourselves through fortnightly meetings, where decisions are taken by Quaker-inspired consensus, though both households — which are vegetarian and non-smoking — are responsible for their own day-to-day practicalities.

To give some idea of our interests, current occupations include theatre production, building, parenting, social research, community work, temping, physical theatre, museum work, psychotherapy, computing, editing, and design.

Uniquely, overall costs are met by members volunteering what they can reasonably contribute within a range centred on the average-per-person income required. Once a year we holiday together to balance the tendencies of city life.

THE NEIGHBOURS COMMUNITY

What kind of people are your members?, you ask. Well, we are Christians, closely linked to local church congregations, Church of England, Quaker, Roman Catholic, and concerned for unity. Joining a residential Christian community is a major counter-cultural step for each of us. Perhaps we are searching for a lifestyle a little nearer to what we know of the early church in Jerusalem, small groups, meeting daily to pray together and support each other in trying to live the Gospel values. They were persecuted by their Roman rulers and although there is no similar persecution for us, we are weakened by the widespread indifference to the Christian faith and strengthened by living closer together.

Rotas? We are full of admiration for the communities which have no rotas and

Year started 1983
Ideological focus christian

Diggers & Dreamers 2004/05

140-148 Ardington Road,
Northampton, NN1 5LT England
Telephone 01604 633918
Electronic Mail neighbours@totalise.co.uk

where the work gets done by whoever is there to do it. We have rotas for prayers and for meals, without which we would sometimes go hungry! Yes, we have a Common Fund into which all pay on a basis pro-rata to earnings. It is a level of sharing which many can accept whereas the financial and emotional demands of a total common purse are only for a few? We think ours is a pattern of community which could happen on any street. Maybe one day it will.

NEW EDUCATION HOUSING CO-OP

The coop owns a traditional end-of-terrace house with mountain views and a long garden. We are located fifteen miles north of Swansea in the Upper Swansea Valley. The outstanding beauty of the Brecon Beacons and the Gower Peninsula Coastline are both nearby, and are easily accessible by public transport. We share housework and bills, food is bought collectively and evening meals are eaten together. Electrical appliances are few by choice (no television, fridge, washing machine), laundry is hand-washed. We promote and practically apply drug-free, tobacco-free and alcohol-free living. We are a member of Radical Routes.

Our current priorities are securing ethical employment for our members and working on future plans. Members pursue varied activities such as promoting liberated parent-

Year started 1986

144

ing, preventing conflict through self-aware-
ness, home-education, healthy eating,
worker and housing co-operatives, collectively owning resources and living lightly.
Visitors are charged only for food and baths.
Please enclose an A5 SAE when first writing
to us.

NEW FUTURES HOUSING CO-OP

Glaneirw is currently home to 8 families (21 people, including 11 kids). The house is full, but we do have room for visitors. Most of us arrived here in the year 2001, and have found that there is a lot of work to be done, both on the house and the land! 'Glaneirw' is an old farm and large mansion house in West Wales surrounded by 46 acres of our own land. It is situated 7 miles north of Cardigan, and is only 2 miles from Ceredigion's beautiful coastline. Most members live in the house, with families sharing rooms, and there are a few people in caravans on the land. The ground floor of the house is communal, and has a kitchen/sitting room, craft room, laundry, kids room, office and library. We try to get most of our food from the land, and there is a large walled garden, an orchard and poly-tunnels for fruit and vegetable growing. We

Year started
Ideological focus ecological

"Glaneirw", Tan-y-Groes,
Cardigan, Ceredigion SA43 2HP Wales
Telephone 01239 810548 **Fax** 01239 810548
Electronic Mail dave@newfutures.fsnet.co.uk

●•

keep goats, chickens and ducks. There is a
mortgage to pay, and most visitors pay an
agreed weekly sum (as do all members) to
cover bills. We all eat one evening meal
together every day, there is a well-equipped
pottery workshop, and a gift shop which we
fill with homegrown produce, eggs and
crafts. We have monthly meetings. Most
chores, including cooking, are shared.
We particularly need carpenters, roofers,
electricians, plasterers, builders, plumbers,
gardeners and alternative energy experts,
but anyone who is willing, with lots of energy and a sense of humour is welcome!
Dogs and other animals by prior arrangement only.
If you would still like to visit, please fill in an
application form. Most visits are for a few
days at first, for your benefit, so that we can
see if we all get along, and if the place is
right for you.

OLD HALL COMMUNITY

Old Hall can be a wonderful, dreadful, exciting, frustrating, friendly, navel-gazing, deeply satisfying place at any time, sometimes all those things at the same time. With 60-odd people of all ages there is an endless permutation of relationships, friendships, bonds, antipathy, harmonies that need working at or occasionally avoiding. Ageing buildings that need constant upkeep, seventy acres of land that provide us with much of our food and endless meals to prepare mean there should never be an empty moment for the committed member. However, we are not isolated from the local community and a fair percentage of adults work outside, mostly part-time in such jobs as teaching, social work, law and engineering, whilst others spend all of their time at Old Hall. The children of school age also go to the local schools.

Year started 1974
Ideological focus ecological

Rectory Hill, East Bergholt,
Colchester, Essex CO7 6TG England
Telephone 01206 298294 **Fax** 01206 299043
Electronic Mail old_hall@btopenworld.com

We believe in making decisions through
consensus and the weekly Friday meetings
can produce lively discussion on a whole
range of topics, from what shape taps to buy
for the toilets to whether we should go solar,
from how often the potato peeler should be
cleaned to whether we should buy non-
organic seed, from where to plant the pars-
ley to a discussion on our raison-d'être.
Dull, it ain't.

PARSONAGE FARM

P arsonage Farm is a community of nine adults and five children about 12 miles from Cambridge. We live in a large old house in three and a half acres of land at the edge of a large village. Most people have absorbing jobs outside the community so the main activity that brings us together is caring for the large organic vegetable garden that supplies most of our vegetarian diet (with occasional fish!). Every third weekend or so we work together with WWOOFers on the garden and we commit ourselves to one week a year of house maintenance. The community has a large Elizabethan barn where there is workshop space and the potential for development of other ideas. We eat together in the evening and support each other informally in childcare and life. The group is quite stable; the most recent member joined over four years

Year started 1971

ago and some members have been here over eighteen years. Some people here work in Delta T Devices, a co-operative business producing electronic research instruments. Delta T was formed by community members 20 years ago and is still going strong, employing 26 at the last count. We are a varied group with interests ranging from re-evaluation counselling to gardening, macrobiotic cooking and music and dance. We like to relax together, particularly in the summer, when barbecues and trips to swim in a local brick pit (and cover ourselves in clay!) are regular features. Our group has been going through a lot of change recently and for the first time for many years we may look for new members. At the moment though we are having a breathing space to take stock and decide where we want to go as a group. We are open to people coming for a weekend visit to garden with us through the WWOOF organisation.

PENNINE CAMPHILL COMMUNITY

●●●●●●●●●●●●●●●●●●●●●●●●●●●●●●●●●

Our main area of work is supporting a college for students with learning disabilities. We're quite a mixed bunch, some who have lived here for twenty years and some who come just for a year to help out. There's always quite an international flavour within the community which we encourage. Co-workers living within the community have their everyday needs met but don't receive a wage. There are also others working at Pennine but living locally. Our farm, garden and traditional craft workshops create unique 'hands on' learning for our students. We are also home to Wakefield Riding for the Disabled, a project we have run jointly for over ten years. We also have two unemployment projects running.

Year started 1977
Ideological focus anthroposophy

Boyne Hill, Chapelthorpe,
Wakefield, West Yorkshire WF4 3JH England
Telephone 01924 255281 **Fax** 01924 240257
Electronic Mail enquiries@pennine.org.uk
World Wide Web http://www.pennine.org.uk

Most of our students are residential and
share our houses on an extended family
basis.
We would like to grow (so much to do) and
welcome people and ideas. Get in touch!

PILSDON COMMUNITY

•••••••••••••••••••••••••••••••••••

The Pilsdon Community was started 40 years ago in this 17th century manor house in a remote part of Dorset. Since then it has welcomed thousands to find a home here, some returning year after year. Guests come from all walks of life and are usually facing some sort of crisis — homelessness, breakdown, addictions etc. We aim for as 'normal' and homely an atmosphere as possible in which guests can take their time to sort out their next step. We do not set an initial limit to a person's stay. We also offer two free nights to wayfarers passing through.

A smallholding of 9 acres with various animals and a large vegetable garden involve guests in sharing in the care and maintenance — always a hoover, spade, paintbrush or hammer at work somewhere! But everyone gets drawn in to muck out the cows'

Year started 1958
Ideological focus christian

Pilsdon Manor,
Bridport, Dorset DT6 5NZ England
Telephone 01308 868308 **Fax** 01308 868161
Electronic Mail pilsden@lineone.net
World Wide Web http://website.lineone.net/~pilsdon

winter quarters! Six (currently) core "members" plus their families (and occasional other volunteers) live in and have responsibility for the Community (not salaried but supported).

We share broadly in a Christian spirituality, participate in daily prayer/meditation and enjoy the privilege of offering hospitality. We are often remembered for our good food! (However, we are by necessity strictly alcohol-free).

PLANTS FOR A FUTURE - CORNWALL

P lants For A Future is a resource centre for rare and unusual plants, particularly those which have edible, medicinal or other uses. We practice vegan-organic permaculture with emphasis on creating an ecologically sustainable environment using perennial plants.

We provide extensive information on 7380 useful plants.

'The Field' is a 28-acre site of Grade II agricultural land on a gentle south-facing slope. This was first planted in 1989 and now has extensive woodland cover and over a thousand different species of plants growing there.

Year started 1989
Ideological focus ecological

The Field, St Veep,
Lostwithiel, Cornwall PL22 0QJ
Telephone 01208 873554
Electronic Mail webmaster@pfaf.org
World Wide Web http://www.pfaf.org

Facilities are basic: there is one agricultural
shed with basic cooking facilities, there is no
electricity and a compost loo.
Most members live in a nearby village.
Visitors will need to camp and are expected
to help work on the site.
PFAF electronic mailing list:
http://groups.yahoo.com/group/pfaf

PLANTS FOR A FUTURE - DEVON

P lants For A Future is a resource centre for rare and unusual plants, particularly those which have edible, medicinal or other uses. We practice vegan-organic permaculture with emphasis on creating an ecologically sustainable environment using perennial plants.

We provide extensive information on 7380 useful plants.

This 84-acre site was bought in July 1997 to form a demonstration garden for useful plants, sustainable agriculture and low-impact living. So far, 20,000 trees have been planted and a number of courses and events have been held.

Facilities are very basic with two mobile homes: one for the visitors centre and one

Year started 1997
Ideological focus ecological

Blagdon Cross, Ashwater,
Beaworthy, Devon EX21 5DF England
Telephone 0845 458 4719
Electronic Mail webmaster@pfaf.org
World Wide Web http://www.pfaf.org

as a unit of accommodation.
We generate all our own electricity, harvest
our own water and use treebogs for toilets.
Visitors will need to camp and are expected
to help work on the site.
PFAF electronic mailing list:
http://groups.yahoo.com/group/pfaf

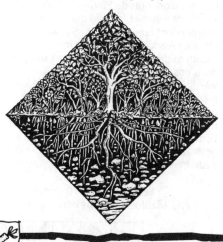

POSTLIP HALL

Postlip Hall is a large, beautiful Grade 1 listed, Jacobean manor house with 15 acres of land, nestling in a quiet valley, surrounded by woods, just below the highest point in the Cotswolds. Currently eight families with ages ranging from almost 1 to 70 plus, most adult inmates work outside Postlip, and although we all eat together fairly frequently, we live independent family lives. Postlip works as a Housing Association, meeting formally every month to discuss, plan, inform and make decisions.

We all pay a monthly ground rent, supplemented by income from the many events we organise both in our magnificent 14th Century tithe barn, from the Cotswold Beer Festival, to barn dances, folk music weekends and wedding celebrations to more intimate musical and dramatic performances in

Year started 1970
Ideological focus none

Postlip Hall, Winchcombe,
Cheltenham, Gloucestershire GL54 5AQ England
Electronic Mail sandymcmillan@careersolutions.co.uk

the main hall.
We work communally in our organic vegetable garden, look after our sheep and
chickens and maintain and improve the
woods, grounds and walls of the estate.
Children are an important part of being here
and thrive in the space and the opportunities that life at Postlip offers them. We all try
to live lightly on the earth and aim to leave
Postlip a
better place
for those
who follow.
You are wel-
come to
visit or
Wwoof, but
please
arrange a
convenient
date with us
first.

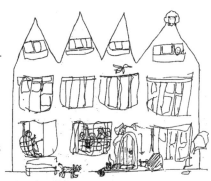

QUAKER COMMUNITY
(BAMFORD)

The Community is nestled amongst trees at the foot of a hill in a beautiful part of the Peak District. Our aim is to enable people to grow together spiritually in a caring environment, living together with a sense of shared adventure.

We look after ten acres of land; some of it is cultivated as organic vegetable gardens and forest gardens. Most of the rest consists of woodland, ponds and a meadow and is managed as our nature reserve. The three families have self-contained accommodation, there are two flats and individuals have bedsits. There are communal rooms in the mainhouse, including a kitchen/dining area where the whole Community can join together for Friday supper and Sunday lunch. We have wheelchair access to the ground floor. On Sundays we host the local Quaker meeting. The Community has no

Year started 1988
Ideological focus quaker

Bamford Quaker Community
Water Lane, Bamford,
Hope Valley, Derbyshire S33 0DA England

hierarchy, and decision making at our weekly house meeting is based on the Quaker business method. Once a month we set aside time to share feelings and reflect on our life together. Members have a variety of occupations outside the Community. We keep pet chickens and goats. Visitors are welcome at some of our working weekends.

RAINBOW HOUSING CO-OPERATIVE

Rainbow (known by many as "The Street") has twenty-four terraced houses in one street situated in the north of Milton Keynes and is in its 23rd year of existence.

The aim of the group is to provide housing in a community setting and there is a communal garden with chickens and ducks (on a pond), organic vegetable growing facilities, play areas for the children and a large barbeque!

The membership, usually between about 30 and 35, with about 20 children of all ages, is very mixed in age, sex and personal circumstances,

One house (No.9) is used as a Community House and has meeting space, office, laundry facilities, a workshop equipped with tools, deep freeze, domestic equipment and greenhouse.

Year started 1977

9 Spencer Street, New Bradwell,
Milton Keynes, Buckinghamshire MK13 0DW England
Telephone 01908 314685

Provision has been made for disabled people with wheel chair access by means of a portable ramp and a toilet suitable for wheelchairs, accessible from indoors and outdoors.

Many members are vegetarian or vegan, although this is not a pre-requisite for membership.

Membership is by application and prospective members are expected to participate in the activities of the co-op, including work days and meetings, before being eligible for membership and therefore housing. It often takes some time before prospective members are successful, as the turnover of houses is infrequent and there are many people waiting.

The co-op is run by general meeting (all members participate in decision making) and most of the maintenance of the property and management of the co-op is done by members.

REDFIELD COMMUNITY

O6.30 - a few smartly-dressed people grunt good morning to each other as they stumble out into the corporate world.

08.00 - Second shift for breakfast. Children dressed neatly in school uniforms eat in varying degrees of vocalised excitement.

09.00 - Day begins for the rest of Redfield. It's a Living in Communities weekend and there are 20 beds to make up in the Centre. There is also lots of work to do in this big Victorian house and on the 17 acre estate. Bob and Mary set off to feed the Jacob sheep. Phil and Dave head off to LILI's office in the Centre. Echos of drums and guitar filter down from the gallery. The smell of baking bread fills the air.

13.00 - Lunch time. People in and out of

Year started 1978
Ideological focus community life

Buckingham Road, Winslow,
Buckingham, MK18 3LZ England
Telephone 01296 713661 **Fax** 01296 714983
Electronic Mail info@redfieldcommunity.org.uk
World Wide Web http://www.redfieldcommunity.org.uk

the kitchen, different jobs to be done. The afternoon flies by ..

15.30 - The house explodes with noise as the children come home from school and are chased out of the kitchen. Cooking for 40 can be stressful!

17.00 - LIC visitors begin to arrive and the house is busier and more vibrant. Lots of new people to meet and greet.

19.00 - Supper in the dining room for a change, mingling with visitors. Everyone pays grateful homage to the cook.

21.00 - Sleepy children in bed, the adults, full of home-grown food and wine, watch Dave's International Communities slide show in the lounge.

24.00 - And so to bed

RUBHA PHOIL FOREST GARDEN

Rubha Phoil, translated from the Gaelic would read Paul's Point, Phoil being Gaelic for Paul, and Rubha, a Point of land, was so named because this 15-acre peninsula was Clan MacDonald land and still is a natural place for landing a boat — which is why it is now the ferry point for the Armadale / Mallaig crossing.

Paul MacDonald, along with his two brothers, made a landfall here after fleeing the massacre of Glencoe.

The brothers settled in this area and we believe Ramsey MacDonald, (the first Labour prime minister), was born here!

The Rhu, as it is called locally, was a place for the community to come and cut peat, and was a gathering place for the clansmen to muster and camp before forays!

Around 1850 the land was planted out with (European) Larch — an essential timber for

Year started 1992
Ideological focus earth-ecological

Armadale Pier Road,
Isle of Skye, IV45 8RS Scotland
Telephone 01471 844700
Electronic Mail sandyru@tiscali.co.uk.
World Wide Web http://www.skye-permaculture.org.uk.

boat building, and most of this was harvested some 60-80 years ago.

Due to being surrounded mainly by water, (therefore sheep and deer being excluded) the land has regenerated naturally with oak, aspen, birch, rowan, sycamore, alder, scots pine, elder, white beam, holly, blackthorn etc. along with a verdant under-storey of indigenous herbs including skullcap, foxglove, many sorrels, pig nut, in fact I haven't enough space to list them all! I must say, however, to visit in May/June is the best time to see the iridescent display of bluebells, then the rhodies, followed by the foxgloves, etc. in what we now have come to regard as our enchanted woodland!

Present: A self-sustainable organic smallholding working on permaculture principles.

Future : Rubha Phoil Retreats ; a tranquil place for paying guests, housed in innovative eco friendly structures.

Opportunities: Loan stock available for the ethical investor.

SALISBURY CENTRE

The Salisbury Centre, the longest established Holistic Centre in Edinburgh, is a large Georgian house with lovely organic gardens, a peaceful haven in the city.

The Centre has offered courses focusing on Spiritual, Emotional and Physical well-being for over 28 years and can provide, at the Centre's direction, occasional overnight accommodation only for participants on many of our courses. The Centre has residential accommodation for up to 6 people and is open to applications as and when positions become available. The accommodation is tied with work in the Centre, running day to day business, gardening, maintenance and housekeeping.

Year started 1973
Ideological focus spiritual

2 Salisbury Road,
Edinburgh, EH16 5AB Scotland
Telephone 0131 667 5438 **Fax** 0131 667 5438
World Wide Web http://www.salisburycentre.org

The heart of our work is to provide an opportunity for growth for anyone seeking to improve the quality of their life through becoming more internally conscious and aware.

The Salisbury Centre celebrates its 30th anniversary in 2003, with a fundraising drive to create a memorial garden in acknowledgement of the 20th anniversary of the passing of its founder Winfred Rushforth.

SANFORD HOUSING CO-OPERATIVE

We have beautiful ponds, gardens and a friendly atmosphere, a tropical communal oasis in London with a famous colourful peace movement mural. Many performers and artists live here and we have tried to artistically redesign our living space.

Founded in 1973, it was built using private finance supplied by the Housing Corporation and Commercial Union. Sanford Housing Co-op consists of 133 units of shared accommodation in 14 purpose-built houses. Its rents are not set by any outside body but are designed to cover actual costs. All the tenants as members of the Co-operative are collectively landlords and responsible for helping the Co-op to protect their interests and to save the Co-op money by their voluntary work.

Sanford actively seeks applicants from all

Year started 1973

11 Sanford Walk,
London, SE14 6NB England
Telephone 020 8692 7316 **Fax** 020 8694 6461
World Wide Web http://www.sanford.i12.com

sections of the community, over the age of 18, who wish to live in a Co-operative, regardless of gender, ethnic origin, disability, sexual orientation or health status.
Sanford is a single person co-operative and is not suitable for applicants who have dependent children or who wish to live as a couple.

SHEKINASHRAM

The Shekinashram is a newly formed spiritual community based upon the precepts of Peace, Unity and Truth. Those who choose to live here have a strong personal commitment to that of deepening self-inquiry, which leads naturally to a respectful relationship with self, life and others. A contemporary blend of eastern and western wisdom is reflected here at the ashram so that each may tread a meaningful path to self-discovery that is relevant in the world today.

We have a group room for hire, and intend to be able to accommodate up to 10 guests on residential workshops as we become more established. We will also have bed and breakfast accommodation available for short and longer term paying guests, and a growing programme of events, workshops, and retreats. We also offer one to one ther-

Year started 2003
Ideological focus spiritual ecological

Dod Lane,
Glastonbury, Somerset BA6 8BZ England
Telephone 0845 4582534
Electronic Mail info@shekinashram.org
World Wide Web http://www.shekinashram.org

apeutic treatments.
As a community we enjoy a primarily vegan
raw food diet and regularly eat together.
We are currently full, however, dependent
upon this changing, we are open to new
members and volunteers who are in align-
ment with our principles. The community is
managed using eco-permaculture principles.
Further details on all of the above are available from us.

SHRUB FAMILY

Our communal name and address is misleading. We are not a farm, don't live in a cottage and if the 'family' brings images of Californian style cults ... we're not a family! We are a practical, secular, dirty-handed, music-playing, screaming kids community. Individual interests range from midwifery and politics to fine arts and drugs legislation. We don't have any particular communal ideal although we follow a pragmatic quest for sustainability and the hope of, one day, developing low-cost, eco-friendly, self-build housing. We share a rambling 17th century farmhouse with room for a maximum of ten to twelve members. We are too small to accommodate communal businesses and most members earn their livings in conven-

Year started 1969
Ideological focus ecological

Shrub Farm Cottages, Larling, East Harling
Norwich, Norfolk NR16 2QT England
Telephone 01953 717844
Electronic Mail timmolly@fast24.co.uk

tional jobs. Although we are surrounded by
beautiful countryside we are close to a busy
road and motor-racing circuit. Combine this
with the presence of two 18-year-old-ish
members and you will see that Shrub is
clearly not a place for those seeking a life of
quiet spiritual contemplation! Our mainly
organic garden and polytunnel give us an
increasing level of self-sufficiency in vegetables. Planting trees, large flower beds and
herbs is a passion. We share communal
costs and dedicate a day's work a week to
the house and grounds. Although we are full
for the forseeable future, we welcome vis-
tors, who should phone first.

SOMEFRIENDS COMMUNITY

●●●●●●●●●●●●●●●●●●●●●●●●●●●●

Fervently eclectic (lively). Hard-edged niceness with cosmic bits. Maybe a little tough sometimes. Challenging, random non-hierarchical. Regular meetings. Comfy consensus. Same monthly rent for all. There are mice, but there is a sliding scale for food. Three floors above a leather shop, East London. Large spacious, rambling. School and prostitutes at back. Many unwilling capitalists. Sesame and Rosie are cats but only one is active at present. And we have our own rooms. Other useful information;

We have 3 eco balls.

300-500 worms some leaving soon with their German girlfriend.

Nice wine appreciated.

Visits can be arranged.

Year started 1973
Ideological focus various

Telephone 020 7739 6824
Electronic Mail Somefriendscommunity@yahoo.com

SPRINGHILL COHOUSING COMMUNITY

•••••••••••••••••••••••••••••••••

Springhill Cohousing is the first new build Cohousing Community in the U.K. and the first project of the Cohousing Development Company. The search for land started in 1999 and the site in Stroud was acquired in 2000. Very soon after, all the plots were pre-sold to members who designed the community and layout of their own houses/flats. During 2003 members will occupy their units.

The principles of Cohousing are concensus decision making, pedestrianised estate, large common house for shared evening meals, private self-contained units.

The 35 houses, flats and studios are super-insulated, 20 houses have 49 Kwp of PV solar panels, there is a car share scheme and the site is Town Centre. There are a number of committees eg. Kitchen, Garden, Parking, Disputes etc. which are mandated to make

Year started 2003
Ideological focus cohousing/consensus

180

Springfield Road,
Stroud, Gloucestershire GL5 1TN England
Telephone 01453 766466
Electronic Mail info@cohouses.net
World Wide Web http://www.cohouses.net

decisions. The idea is to reduce the number
of large meetings and trust small groups to
make decisions.

Joining is by self selection. The only criteria
are that the new members agree with the
principles of Cohousing and can afford to
buy in. Three units have an inbuilt 15%
"affordability" discount.

COMMUNITY OF ST FRANCIS

The Community of St. Francis is an Active community in the Franciscan tradition in the Church of England. Central to our life is the commitment to regular corporate and personal prayer and study which undergirds hospitality, mission and caring work.

At Compton Durville the sisters receive guests, normally for a maximum of 6 days, for rest, retreat and holidays. Up to 18 resident guests and day groups of up to 65 can be accommodated. The sisters share a common dining room with guests, and chapel services are open to all. A programme of Quiet Days and retreats, including individually guided retreats is offered. As a registered charity there is no fixed charge for guests but a contribution is requested.

Other houses of the community are in urban priority areas where small groups of

Year started 1905
Ideological focus christian

St Francis Convent, Compton Durville,
South Petherton, Somerset TA13 5ES England
Telephone 01460 240473 **Fax** 01460 242360
Electronic Mail comptondurvillecsf@franciscans.org.uk
World Wide Web http://www.franciscans.org.uk

sisters are in part-time semi-vocational,
sometimes salaried work. The community
has no major funds and members have to
assist in generating sufficient income.

Community members make traditional religious vows of poverty, celibate
chastity, and obedience, endeav-
ouring to live these out in an
open spirit of life sharing and
relationships. Decision making
is mutual,
consultative
and where
possible by
consensus.
An elected
chapter and
officers oper-
ate as appro-
priate.

STEPPING STONES
HOUSING CO-OP

Stepping Stones Housing Co-op was formed in 1999 with the intention of providing secure, ecologically friendly housing to its members in a rural setting where people could live in a non hierarchical community. Highbury Farm is a 30-acre smallholding with a large farmhouse, extensive outbuildings, mobile homes and the possibility of low impact structures.

The land comprises mainly of pasture, which has greater conservation than agricultural value, though we have an historic, productive orchard and space for vegetable production. We also host camps and gatherings in our fields.

We are situated above the incredibly beautiful Wye Valley, surrounded by woodland nature reserves, but are not isolated from

Year started 1999
Ideological focus ecological

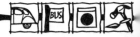

local amenities and are integrated into the local community. At the moment we are trying to grow at a sustainable rate to form a stable, committed community of about 12 adults. We aim to be child-friendly, and to give consideration to their needs. Accommodation is in the main house, in caravans or vehicles, but a variety of other options can be explored You are welcome to visit, but please arrange this beforehand. We ask for a small contribution towards food and bills. Arrival by public transport is encouraged.

STEWARD COMMUNITY WOODLAND (AFFINITY)

We are seven woodland dwellers (including a toddler) enjoying living and working in a 32 acre mixed woodland on the edge of Dartmoor. We are running a permaculture project to demonstrate the value of integrating conservation woodland management (such as coppicing and broadleaf planting) with organic growing, traditional skills and crafts, and low-impact sustainable living.

We are living in bender-style, timber frame and earth sheltered dwellings, which include the communal Longhouse and Kitchen. And there's a treehouse too! We have a micro hydro scheme and solar panels to generate electricity, from which we run lighting, computers and even an electric chainsaw. There's a communal van run on biodiesel.

Year started 2000
Ideological focus ecological

Moretonhampstead,
Newton Abbot, Devon TQ13 8SD England
Telephone 01647 440233 **Fax** 07050 674 467
Electronic Mail affinity@stewardwood.org
World Wide Web http://www.stewardwood.org

● ●

We spend our time gardening, coppicing,
conifer felling and native tree planting,
maintaining and improving our dwellings
and infrastructure, running courses, on out-
reach work (such as cycle-powered workshops), and on working for social change.
We have a large veg growing area and
young forest garden. We are a vegan community and so do not have any livestock.
We have been granted planning permission
for five years to live here and continue the
project (subject to various conditions). We
welcome visitors for short or long stays
(please phone first to arrange this) although
cannot do so on a WWOOFing basis. And
we're looking for new members. Finally, we
have a large, lively website that has our
latest news and events alongside 'how to'
guides, a photo gallery and more.

TALAMH

Our ideological approach is one of environmental sustainability. We have 10 members, two children and two teenagers living here. We either live in the farmhouse, or on the land in caravans. We have horses, dogs, cats, chickens and lots of wildlife about.

The co-op is set in 50 acres of land which provides the base for an environmental charity, Talamh Life Centre. The charity runs regular working weeks in such activities as tree planting and organic gardening and other workshops. Visitors to the co-op are welcomed as volunteers.

All meals are vegetarian (can be vegan) and communal, and food and some chores are carried out on a rota basis. Minimal donations to cover food and board are welcomed.

Year started 1993
Ideological focus environmental

Birkhill House,
Coalburn, Lanarkshire ML11 0NJ Scotland
Telephone 01555 820400 **Fax** 01555 820400
Electronic Mail talamh@lineone.net
World Wide Web http://website.lineone.net/~talamh

Accommodation is basic, in a bunk room and may be shared, if during a working week. Heating is by wood burners. Sometimes a visitor's caravan is available. For people with children we can time your visit so that you have a space to yourselves, if you contact us in advance.

Visitors are welcome to stay here for up to 2 weeks. Contact us in advance so that we can book a space for you. We are a non-profit making group, and a host for "WWOOF".

Decisions in the co-op are made by consensus, and members usually meet weekly to discuss any agendas and communal workdays. We welcome volunteers of all backgrounds, and appreciate all contributions of help offered to our community.

TANGRAM HOUSING CO-OP

Tangram is a registered Housing Co-operative. We have 40 units of accommodation, all in or near Bank Side Street in Harehills, Leeds. They range from studio flats through to four-bedroom family houses. We also have some communal accommodation. We are funded by the Housing Corporation (a government body), which means that we are regulated and can afford to keep our houses in a high state of repair.

The Co-op is run by the tenants with support from a part-time worker. All tenants are members of the co-operative and have to be voted in at a General Meeting.

As a tenant, you enjoy the following advantages: cheap rent (about £33 per week for a one-bed flat), a centrally heated flat or house, a great repairs service, training and advice if you need it, the control of being

Year started 1978
Ideological focus co-operative

76 Bank Side Street,
Leeds, West Yorkshire LS8 5AD England
Telephone 0113 248 8743
Electronic Mail info@tangramhousing.org.uk

your own landlord, and a friendly and welcoming community that cares for its members.
In return for this, we expect you to spend about 2 hours a week helping to run the Co-op. As well as keeping rents down, this is a great way of socialising with the other Co-op members.

TARALOKA BUDDHIST RETREAT CENTRE FOR WOMEN

Taraloka is both a community and a Buddhist retreat centre for women, to which women come from all over the world to experience the calm, beautiful atmosphere which has built up over the fifteen years of the centre's existence.

All of us living here are committed to Buddhist ideals and to creating the best possible facilities for women to come on retreat. For the purposes of our work, the community is divided into two teams, the Retreat Team and the Support Team, with one retired member.

We all actively pursue the Buddhist way of life, following a daily programme of meditation, work and communal meals. There is a strong emphasis on ethical practice, aiming for more kindness, generosity, contentment,

Year started 1983
Ideological focus buddhist

truthful speech and clarity of mind. Apart from our respective team meetings, we hold weekly community meetings and business meetings. We aim to be friendly and cooperative and decisions are arrived at through consensus.

Taraloka is registered as a charity and all members receive the same basic support. We are all part of the Buddhist Movement of the FWBO (Friends of the Western Buddhist Order) and mainly offer retreats for people who have had some experience within that movement. We also run Newcomers Weekends where we introduce meditation and Buddhism and there is an Open Day each year.

For further information please contact our secretary.

TORCH HOUSING CO-OP

We're a Housing Co-operative that's been around for over 7 years, a mile or so away from the city centre in what is one of the most culturally diverse cities in Britain.

We arose from the Radical Student population of the early 1990's via New Education Housing Co-op and are members of Radical Routes and take part in an awful lot of different things.

We've got 2 big, beautiful houses 100 yds away from each other, one a 5-bedroom Georgian Style and the other an 8-bedroom Grade II listed mansion with office space and a big community room, both of which we rent out to other organisations or else use ourselves for parties, meetings etc.

We are a lively group of people that like living collectively and are very diverse in ages, views and diet, but very definitely are

Year started 1994
Ideological focus humanitarian

10 Richmond Road, Hockley,
Birmingham, West Midlands B18 5NH England
Telephone 0121 554 4256
Electronic Mail jantorch@aol.com / Jantorch1@Tiscali.co.uk

alternative.
Our kitchens are collectively Vegetarian and
communal meals are optional and arise
spontaneously, along with our parties.
We are always looking for new members to
help us run everything and to replace the
ones that have moved on and if you would
like to find out more, drop us a line. We are
also open to visitors and friends popping in,
but ring us first.

TOWNHEAD COLLECTIVE

Townhead Collective is made up of around 23 adults, 7 kids, 6 dogs, 9 chickens and one hard-core cat. We have 19 old railway cottages with 3.5 acres of land in rural Yorkshire.

The Community has been formed by a collection of environmental protesters, travellers, locals and squatters. We are into growing our own organic fruit and veg, producing all our own electricity and composting all our own poo.

We have two large communal gardens with polytunnels, herb garden and a tree nursery. All our leccy comes from solar, wind and soon hydropower.

Since 1998 we have been renovating the semi-derelict houses and have learnt and shared many skills.

Year started 1998
Ideological focus ecological

care of Diggers & Dreamers

The atmosphere is informal, friendly and relaxed. We only have meetings when we have to and the only rota is for dog-poo scooping.
We all have our personal spaces as well as communal areas including living room, pool room, office with internet access, workshops, kids room and kitchen.
Communal meals are cooked daily for £2.50.
Visitor's space is available and extra helping hands are always appreciated.
We respect each other's opinions, have good parties, do more recycling than Brambles, drink more beer than Talamh and are proud winners of the Inter-Community Volleyball Golden Bum award.

TULLYCOLL TRUST FOUNDATION

We, at the foundation, are committed to a living life process of making our contribution to an enlightened planetary civilization by demonstrating the following principles:

- Suppressed emotions and limiting thoughts can safely be expressed and released.
- By releasing suppressed emotions and limiting thoughts, we can let go of self-defeating patterns and experience transformation.
- All feelings are valid
- Everyone is inherently lovable and innocent
- Everyone is responsible for their own personal experience
- Regardless of appearances, there are only two emotions, love and fear, and all actions unlike love are cries for help.
- Mistakes are for correction, not punishment

Year started 1994
Ideological focus based on 'A Course in Miracles'

Tullycoll House , 10 Tullycoll Road,
Cookstown, Co Tyrone BT80 9QY, Northern Ireland
Telephone 028 86758785 **Fax** 028 86758815
Electronic Mail Tullycoll@hotmail.com

We believe that the message of spirit
throughout the world is the same. It is a
message of love, tolerance, compassion,
respect, optimism and a profound understanding of community.

The Tullycoll Trust Foundation is an open
fellowship of people united by commitment
to spiritual growth and a desire to support
themselves and others in a safe, loving environment, thereby creating a safer, loving
planet.

The Foundation is based on the belief that
spiritual development and leadership is
accelerated and more effective within the
safety and ongoing support of a committed
group. Leadership and direction are provided by an association of Spiritual Leaders and
Teachers of a Course in Miracles.

THE WELL AT WILLEN

The Well is a large house in 3 acres of land located on the outskirts of Milton Keynes, next to Willen Lake. The community which was founded in 1997 has grown from a Christian base, however we welcome as members people of differing beliefs. Each family/individual has their own living space as well as sharing in the communal areas. We currently have seven adult residential members and five children. We are looking for new members.

As community members we aim to have a daily, shared meal and one act of reflection/prayer together, which is led by a different member of the community each week in accordance with their own beliefs. The daily tasks of the community (cooking,

Year started 1997
Ideological focus ecumenical

The Well, Newport Road, Willen
Milton Keynes, Buckinghamshire MK15 9AA England
Telephone 01908 242190 **Fax** 01908 242187
Electronic Mail community@thewellatwillen.org.uk
World Wide Web http://www.thewellatwillen.org.uk

cleaning, shopping) are based on a rota
system. We are a housing co-operative. We
all pay rent on our private living quarters
and contribute towards food each week.
In choosing to live together we offer an
alternative to the prevailing trend of individ-
ualism. We offer hospitality and seek to
promote Peace and Justice: this takes many
forms including a project to support local
asylum seekers.

WOODHEAD COMMUNITY

●●●●●●●●●●●●●●●●●●●●●●●●●●●●●●●●●●●

Woodhead is continually evolving. It began with a vision and focus of being a land and family based spiritual community. Eight years on, these original elements are more or less still in place and we have broadened our perspective to include the needs and visions of the many people of different nationalities who have lived here. Our passions, skills and aspirations are as varied as the members. The spiritual dimension is central to us, but as an individual and personal practice, rather than as a collective one.

Currently we are making space for personal creative expression. Maintaining and working with relationship is what gives juice to our community.

Currently we consist of two families, and four single adults. We have five children between us. We live in beautiful surround-

Year started 1994
Ideological focus Collectively Living with Spirit

Kinloss,
Forres, Moray IV36 2UE Scotland
Telephone 01309 674000 **Fax** 01309 674000
Electronic Mail hugh@woodheadcom.org

ings, valuing our garden, the local countryside and our close proximity to the Findhorn
Foundation. We eat together at least five
nights a week, enjoying home-grown food
and companionship. We have a weekly
sharing/business meeting. Discussions can
be intense, fun and challenging at the same
time. We are changing to a more collectively
owned structure, though we have yet to
decide on the format. When space is available we are open to visitors and prospective
new members.

WOOLMAN HOUSE

We are a small community offering hospitality to refugees in inner-city Liverpool. We began by befriending a Kosovan family, then helped to set up a drop-in for refugees and a group visiting immigration detainees in Liverpool Prison. In 2002 we opened our 'house of hospitality', sharing our home with a destitute asylum-seeker and offering overnight lodging to others coming to Liverpool for asylum interviews.

In doing this we try to practise the Christian tradition of hospitality to the stranger and outcast. Our name remembers John Woolman, the 18th Century Quaker slavery abolitionist, whose Journal advocates a simple and nonviolent way of life. We are also inspired by the Catholic Worker movement and its founders Peter Maurin and Dorothy Day, who believed that Christians should

Year started 1999
Ideological focus christian

204

care of Diggers & Dreamers
Telephone 0151 281 5894

'comfort the afflicted and afflict the comfort-able.' We are not a charity, nor do we accept state funding, but we support our-selves through paid work and are in turn supported by a strong network of volunteers and friends.

Our work is inevitably small in scale, but offers we hope a sign of the solidarity and sharing that char-acterise the reign of God. We pub-lish a newsletter, 'Sanctuary', and lead meditative prayer in the Taize style once a month in a local church.

ZION HOUSING CO-OP

We purchased the 'Nutclough Tavern' thanks to the Co-op Bank and Radical Routes, in December 2002.

Our housed members are four men and four women, no couples, frequently visited by varied partners and assorted children. Between us we're involved in arts, crafts, computing, healing, performing arts, perma-culture, gardening/trees stuff and teaching. The Co-op also provides cheap meeting and office space to local groups.

We believe that the co-operative structure can enable people to take control of their housing/working in an empowering way, giving some security and support, whilst allowing energy to be poured into positive work towards personal, social and ecological change. We hold weekly house meetings

Year started 2002

Nutclough Tavern, 6-8 Nutclough,
Hebden Bridge, West Yorkshire HX7 8HA England
Electronic Mail info@zionhousingco-op.com
World Wide Web http://www.zionhousingco-op.com

and monthly general co-op meetings with decisions by consensus.

Our buildings and garden are a work in progress. We're creating our fruit and veg growing around outdoor performance/healing/playing space. We are building more bedrooms, a large communal kitchen, a practical 'messy' workshop and a fully accessible studio/workshop with a toilet and kitchen to share.

Oh, and the sauna, hot tub, summerhouse, mini labyrinth and earth oven. Check our website for details.

It's great living in this old pub, in busy, buzzy, lovely Hebden Bridge. Hard work and very worthwhile. WWOOFers and paying adult guests welcome for 2-7 days with one month notice.

AMADEA COHOUSING COMMUNITIES

30 The Front, Potten End,
Berkhamsted, Hertfordshire HP4 2QR England
Telephone 01442 874187 **Fax** 01442 874187
Electronic Mail home@deliadudgeon.go-plus.net

Amadea, in its present form evolved from an article appearing in "Resurgence" magazine some nine years ago entitled "Three Score Years and Then?" Its early focus was on a purpose built 'centre' for people in the last third of life, but other associated avenues were explored. It is now a network of people and groups meeting locally to develop plans for community living with a spiritual focus. There is a centrally held depository of information and experience available to groups developing their own schemes and a regular Newsletter. We want to make our lives together creative, healing and fun.

We come from various walks of life but share a vision of community life which involves a deep concern for the planet and all who live on it. Many of us would like to employ permaculture principles. Some groups will build from scratch, others convert existing properties, with a range of possibilities for ownership or renting. Each group will develop its own guidelines and focus within the Amadea ideology, but is likely to have a shared sacred space, meeting room and shared use of utilities.

Ideological focus ecological

ANARRES

c/o Blackcurrent, 24 St.Michael's Ave, Northampton, NN1 4JQ
Telephone 0845 458 8259
Electronic Mail blackcurrent@lineone.net

We are a forming community, which intends to establish an ecovillage, in (or next to) a wood. Our main concerns and plans are: to help demonstrate that people can exist happily and healthily without degrading the environment, and that human communities are sustainable living elements of the natural world; to grow food and other useful plants veganically; a nonviolent philosophy; shared childcare; no motorised vehicles; preferably near to a Sustrans route; no livestock, pets or rescued animals; income pooling; doing without electricity, gas, fossil fuels or concrete. We don't want to move to the wood until we have a confident group of six to ten people who have lived together for at least a year at Blackcurrent (see separate entry).

We are especially looking for people with skills and experience in: woodcraft (esp. green wood); building with wattle and daub, wood and stone; well building without bricks; dentistry; forest gardening; no-dig veganic food production; coppicing; reed beds; clay woodstoves; making fabric and dyes from plants; clog making; plant and fungi identification. However, if none of this sounds like you, but you're enthusiastic, willing to learn and you share similar dreams to ours, please get in touch anyway.

Ideological focus nonviolence

CO-HOUSING BRISTOL

c/o 20 Cornwall Road, Bishopston, Bristol, BS7 8LH
Telephone 0117 9422569
Electronic Mail abigail@spring96.freeserve.co.uk
WWW http://groups.yahoo.com/group/bristolcohousing

We are an embryonic co-housing group that has been meeting since June 2001. We intend to purchase land within a 15-mile radius of Bristol, large enough to accomodate up to 35 households.

We are currently a mixture of households with and without children, singles and couples. We actively encourage people of all ages and backgrounds to be part of our group, and join our monthly meetings, which deal with business and also offer the opportunity for people to get to know each other better.

Our intention is to build or convert individual properties (low impact and energy efficient) that can be owned, rented or part-owned/part-rented, depending on individual choice and the availability of partnership funding.

There will be a communal building with shared resources. We want the main area of the site to be vehicle-free, with green space for children to roam freely and safely.

Some of us are keen to grow vegetables, keep animals, set up co-operative businesses and provide workshop space to rent. We want to be outward-looking and seek ways to involve and engage with the wider community.

COHOUSING 2000, EDINBURGH

care of Diggers & Dreamers

◆ ● ● ◆ ● ◆ ◆ ● ● ● ◆ ● ● ● ● ◆ ◆ ● ● ◆ ● ● ● ◆ ◆ ◆ ● ● ◆ ●

We're currently a fairly small (but still enthusiastic and very much determined) group from a variety of backgrounds ranging in age from one and a half to sixty something. Our plan is to design and build Scotland's first Cohousing neighbourhood of between 15 and 25 houses in the Edinburgh area. We will all have our own self-contained homes but the overall design of the neighbourhood will specifically aim to foster community. A key feature will be the inclusion of a jointly-owned common house and gardens. We hope to include communal cooking and eating areas, workshop and office space, children's play area and guest bedrooms in our common house. Residents will be involved in the planning and design of the neighbourhood and will jointly manage the scheme once it is built. We intend to mix private, rented and shared-ownership homes. Our community will be non-ideological and we will build to the highest environmental standards. We meet once a month or so and would welcome new members.Securing a site has proved a major challenge with many disappointments.

However, we are now focusing on getting land in a proposed new development in the south east of Edinburgh. Please contact us to find out more!

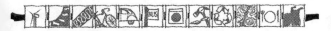

COLNE VALLEY CO-HOUSING PROJECT

care of Diggers & Dreamers

T he Colne Valley CoHousing Project is developing an innovative and sustainable housing and living project. We have come together out of a shared desire to collaborate in creating a mutually supportive community, putting into practice the values of mutual support, co-operation and a concern for the local and global environment. We want to live in a way which will allow us to enjoy each other's company, work together, have fun, innovate, be inspired and be inspiring to others.

The project intends to create a mini-neighbourhood of 8-10 households. Each household having their own private dwelling while also enjoying the use of, and being committed to, a wide range of complementary communal facilities managed by the whole group. The group is interested in undertaking some self-build and is committed to using ecological building technologies.

The project will take place in the Colne Valley, West Yorkshire. The group is focusing on securing a site at the western, more rural, end of the valley close to the small Pennine towns of Marsden and Slaithwaite.

Ideological focus ecological

CURNEY BANK COMMONWEALTH

Curney Bank Wood, Newcastle on Clun,
Craven Arms, Shropshire SP7 8PW
Electronic Mail david.gillen@curney.fsnet.co.uk

We are converting our 33-acre ex-Forestry Commission plantation (purchased in 2000) to agro-forestry or forest farming. We produce and sell free range chicken, pork, bacon and smoked duck. All livestock play an integral role in the management of the land e.g. pigs root out existing weeds and prepare the ground for planting forage crops and trees. Wwoofers are welcome.

Future

We intend to purchase a farm and divide it into an appropriate number of smallholdings to form a commonwealth and build low-cost housing. Ownership of land and housing will be vested in the commonwealth. Prospective members must be able to demonstrate their commitment to high welfare livestock production - membership invitation achieved by working on existing holding.

ORCHARD LAND TRUST & DRAGON HOUSING CO-OP

care of Diggers & Dreamers
Telephone 0845 330 5034
Electronic Mail michelle.virgo@i12.com

We are a group of six adults and six children (five home educated) who are committed to living sustainable lifestyles in Southeast Cornwall. We intend that a non-profit company will purchase land, which will be held in trust, individuals will be unable to sell land or assets for speculative gain. Our ideal piece of land would be in excess of 10 acres and close to public transport links. It would have good access, some woodland and some gently southward sloping growing land, maybe with a spring or two and a stream running along one edge. Management of the land will follow permaculture principles. Through Dragon Housing Co-op we intend to build affordable, autonomous, low-impact homes, constructed wherever possible, using local, biodegradable and recycled materials. We envisage that many of us will be employed on the land in organic horticulture, crafts or education.

We would like to hear from you if you have a commitment to sustainable land use and low impact living, if you have some time, energy and money to invest and if you're willing to learn, grow and celebrate with us.

214

SOUTH HAMS HOLISTIC EDUCATION COMMUNITY

10a Riverside,
Totnes, Devon TQ9 5JB England
Telephone 01803 868744
Electronic Mail cj.rees@virgin.net

W e are a group of families and individuals wishing to adopt a way of life that's eco-sustaining, mutually loving and beneficial. We are already running a practical course on self-build eco-home building and sustaining energy systems which has been subsidised by a grant from the European Social Fund. This is the first of a range of workshops and courses we will eventually run, as the members of our Community have a wide diversity of skills to pass on to the greater world: Holistic Health and Healing: Permaculture design: eco-architecture and energy systems, gardening, various arts and music, sacred geometry, pottery, joinery and frame building etc.

In 2003 we hope to buy a large farm house with barns and land to have as our centre and build or convert about six eco-homes there. It will be in South Hams, in the Totnes area. New members or Associates are welcome to join, especially if they have some capital to offer. Both members and Associates have a £1 nominal share giving them the co-ownership rights, (if Member) and access to our facilities if they are a non-residential Associate, and one vote in General Meetings on policy.

Ideological focus self & eco-sustaining educational

VEGAN ENTERPRISE

c/o 31 Caerau Road, Caerau, Maesteg
Bridgend, Mid Glamorgan CF34 0PB Wales
Telephone 01656 739813
Electronic Mail robert-howes@totalise.co.uk

Vegan Enterprise covers: Vegan Enterprises Ltd, the Vegan Community Project and a number of planned, community run, projects and businesses, and is being run in conjunction with Brynderwen Vegan Community (see their entry). It takes over from the previous entry, The Prometheus Project.

The plan is to create jobs (especially for non-smoking vegans) and to create the conditions for change on a community scale and subsequently on a larger scale. There is already one full time worker, and the early possibility of several more positions. We are not afraid to do what needs to be done in order to help create a better world, that is; a non-violent approach to a non-violent world.

We had planned to move to Devon but are, for the moment, developing the South Wales branch. A planned timeshare business could prove pivotal in the acquisition of land and property in this country and various other countries.

Ideological focus ecobusiness

WELHEALTH

care of Diggers & Dreamers

 ● ❂

You can only exchange something if it is scarce. Price is dependent on scarcity. Land to grow food is not scarce, it has been made scarce. That's murder. That's why we're diggers.

If there is sufficient, enough to go around and everyone has access to it, there's no demand, it will be PRICELESS and FREE. If you make money selling food, you are making money off the back of a purposeful starvation of people, creating scarcity in an abundant world.

If you make money out of other things, which are not bare necessities, you are only able to do this because advances in energy efficiency of work throughout the ages have made agricultural workers progressively unemployed and they seek things to make and sell back to the employed agricultural workers and land owner. Thus you are also complicit in the murder of scarcity of life's needs.

We are down-shifting, co-operative, anti-consumerist, vegan diggers and wombles, we have land to create alternative, renewable, sharing, Forest Garden Farms.

Ideological focus forest garden diggers wombles

CATALYST COLLECTIVE

Vectis, Wyesham Avenue, ,
Monmouth, NP25 3NF Wales
Telephone 01600 775414
Electronic Mail catalyst@co-op.org
World Wide Web http://www.eco-action.org/catalyst\

°°°°°°°°°°°°°°°°°°°°°°°°°°°°°°°°°°°°

Catalyst Collective Ltd is a worker co-operative. We help people set up and register co-ops and in the last ten years over 100 housing co-ops, about 30 worker co-ops, a couple of charities, and a variety of different companies with co-operative aims have been registered through catalyst. We have worked with various existing co-ops, as well as groups intending to set up co-ops; on issues such as group-working, legal structures, conflict resolution, financial viability of proposals, co-operation and meeting skills etc. Basically, we love working with and promoting co-ops (especially ethical & eco-friendly ones), and have a wide variety of skills & knowledge available. We also actively encourage co-operation between groups of various types, and Catalyst is a member of (or actively involved with) Radical Routes, ICOM, ICOF, Confederation of Co-operative Housing, UK Co-operative Council, and The Co-op Party. If your group is considering setting up as a co-op, we can usually arrange for someone to come to speak to you. Please contact us if this would be useful. Obviously, where possible, we'd like to be paid for our work & time, but we enjoy our work so, as long as our travel costs are covered, we'll probably be happy to work with you (whether you can afford to pay us or not!).We are here to help - and if you have a query, don't hesitate to contact us.

THE COHOUSING DEVELOPMENT COMPANY

16 Springhill Cohousing Community, Stroud, Gloucestershire
GL5 1TN England **Fax** 01453 751919
Electronic Mail info@cohouses.net
World Wide Web http://www.cohouses.net

ᗡᗡᗡᗡᗡᗡᗡᗡᗡᗡᗡᗡᗡᗡᗡᗡᗡᗡᗡᗡᗡᗡᗡᗡᗡᗡᗡᗡᗡᗡᗡᗡ

T he Cohousing Company built the first new-build Cohousing Community in Stroud (see Springhill Cohousing entry). It is about to start the second. Please check the website for up to date details. Members join during the design stage and exchange contracts on their chosen plot either for a flat or house. We are negotiating on buying sites in Stroud, Milton Keynes and elsewhere. Please email if you wish to join (say something about yourself).

If we are still looking and if you know of a suitable site for sale please let us know by email.

The principles of Cohousing are that decisions are made by consensus, the site is pedestrianised, the large common house is used for shared meals and is an extension to members' private self-contained units — and if you have a query, don't hesitate to contact us.

CONFEDERATION OF CO-OPERATIVE HOUSING

Unit 19, 41 Old Birley Street, Hulme, Manchester, M15 5RF
Telephone 0161 232 1588 **Fax** 0161 226 7307
Electronic Mail info@cch.coop
World Wide Web http://www.cch.coop

The Confederation of Co-operative Housing is the national representative body for co-operative housing in England + Wales. We are run entirely by volunteers representing member co-ops. CCH was set up in 1993 to promote, support and lobby all forms of community controlled and co-operative housing: tenant management in social housing, leaseholder co-ops, community land trusts as well as ownership co-ops. CCH works closely with Co-operatives UK, and after over a decade is now considered a suitable consultee on much national housing policy with government departments and the Housing Corporation.

We work towards the day when:
• All tenants and residents can determine how their neighbourhoods are run
• All those who wish will be able to manage and own their homes through democratic membership organisations
• Housing associations provide services to community controlled organisations.
• Tenants and residents will lead the dialogue with government about housing provision.

ECO-VILLAGE NETWORK FOR THE UK

PO Box 1410, Bristol, BS99 3JP England
Electronic Mail evnuk@gaia.org
World Wide Web
http://www.ecovillages.org/uk/network/index.html

◊◊◊◊◊◊◊◊◊◊◊◊◊◊◊◊◊◊◊◊◊◊◊◊◊◊◊◊◊◊◊◊

E VNUK is the UK branch of Global Eco-Village Network. We aim to encourage and help enable people and organisations in developing environmentally, socially and economically sustainable settlements. We promote sustainable settlement for all by acting as an information resource and news service and by maintaining a website listing eco-village projects, skills and resources. We provide current information on eco-village theories and practices, alternative technologies and sponsor workshops and events in order to increase public awareness of the issues.

THE FAMILY

Maxet House, Liverpool Rd,
Luton, LU1 1RS England
Telephone 01582 450166
Electronic Mail info@thefamilyeurope.org
World Wide Web http://www.thefamily.org/thefamily

◇◇◇◇◇◇◇◇◇◇◇◇◇◇◇◇◇◇◇◇◇◇◇◇◇◇◇◇◇◇◇◇

The Family (formerly known as the Children of God) is an international Christian movement, active in over 100 countries. Our fulltime members live in communal homes with an average of around 12 members. Our goal is to put true love into action, in fulfilment of what Jesus said, "the two greatest commandments ... are to love God ... and to love your neighbour as yourself" (Matthew 22:37-40). Each community is self-governing, deciding its own specific activities. Our centre in Luton can give an introduction to the Family -- our beliefs, lifestyle and activities. Visits can also be arranged at our communal homes; it's up to the decision of the homes' residents.

COMMUNITIES OF L'ARCHE

10 Briggate, Silsden,
Keighley, Yorkshire BD20 9JT England
Telephone 01535 656186 **Fax** 01535 656426
Electronic Mail info@larche.org.uk
World Wide Web www.larche.org.uk

◊◊◊◊◊◊◊◊◊◊◊◊◊◊◊◊◊◊◊◊◊◊◊◊◊◊◊◊◊

I n L'Arche, people with and without learning disabilities share home life in ordinary houses, like any family. Shopping, cooking, sharing a meal — through these simple daily things, people learn and grow.

They become friends, part of a network of people sharing their lives together. Some may come from institutional care, others from their families. Some need more support than others. Some come because of their commitment to helping people with learning disabilities. Each seeks to live in a real home, as a responsible adult, in equal relationship with others.

People feel good in achieving something, however small. Most L'Arche communities offer skilled work, therapy and training in community craft and horticulture workshops. Some members are supported to take up open employment, to attend college, or to attend local day services. Older members are helped to find new interests in their retirement years.

L'Arche is ecumenical, rooted in the Christian tradition, welcoming and respecting people whatever their personal beliefs. Its communities bring together people who have diverse interests and abilities, from different cultures, nationalities, denominations and faiths. All are encouraged to deepen in spirituality according to their own traditions.

RADICAL ROUTES

16 Sholebroke Avenue, Chapeltown,Leeds, LS7 3HB
Telephone 0113 262 9365
Electronic Mail cornerstone@gn.apc.org
WWW http://www.radicalroutes.org.uk

◊◊◊◊◊◊◊◊◊◊◊◊◊◊◊◊◊◊◊◊◊◊◊◊◊◊◊◊◊◊◊◊◊◊◊◊◊

Radical Routes is a network of radical co-ops working for social change. It is an independent secondary co-op formed by independent primary co-operatives. The day-to-day operation of Radical Routes is funded by service payments from its member co-operatives, by interest on loans and by donations. Money invested in Radical Routes is used to provide loans to its members. The members are currently registered housing and worker co-operatives actively working towards social change, but we are in the process of expanding to include other groups (eg radical social centres). Each co-operative participates in the running of the organisation, each has one vote and is fully involved in decision making. Finance is raised through the sale to individuals and businesses of shares in Rootstock, the ethical investors' co-op which only invests in Radical Routes.

Radical Routes publishes "How to Set Up a Housing Co-op" and "How to Set Up a Workers Co-op" for £2.50 each, and a Directory of Member Co-ops and Introduction to Radical Routes for £1.50 each. Well-hidden cash or cheques/PO made payable to Radical Routes should be sent to the enquiries address. Enquiries about ethical investment in Rootstock to:Zion Housing Co-op, Nutclough Tavern, Kieghley Road, Hebden Bridge, West Yorkshire, tel: 07960 055 846 or 01422 845990; email: info@zionhousingco-op.com

VEGAN COMMUNITY NETWORK

c/o Heart Sing 2 Seaview Terrace, Tydraw, Bonymaen
Swansea, SA1 7BD Wales
Telephone 01792 476737

The Vegan Community Network is a loose coalition of vegans who share a common interest in intentional community. Some of us see eye-to-eye as to what shape or form a community should take, some of us hold wildly differing dreams from each other.

At the time of writing there is interest in an 11-bedroom hotel in Swansea to be bought possibly by a small group of us. Malcolm Horne (01395 270280) remains interested in buying this hotel or another collective building to make accommodation and social space for vegans. More joiners with funds to add may be welcomed. Malcolm at present organises Devon Vegans and also runs the annual Vegan National Gathering.

Bob Howes (01656 739813 robert-howes@totalise.co.uk) prefers to concentrate upon businesses 'for vegans and potential vegans', principally recycling and vegan organic horticulture, but also property/accommodation. A piece of land in Devon and two houses in South Wales are already available.

Frank Bowman (07980 158661) has been responsible for the long-running Give-and-Take stall at Connahs Quay market. There is a group possibly emerging who are interested in 'own front doors' in a 'village' setting.

We set up Vegan Hotels Ltd, a company that makes sharing ('shares in') a property easier.

Please e-mail us if you'd like our future URL.

Want to Support Community Living?

The **Revolving Loan** is an unsecured loan which is lent to any intentional community. The present loan is for £1,000 and is with Earthworm Housing Co-op to help with roofing work. To help create more and bigger revolving loans, we need more donations (however small – it all helps!).

If you would like to contribute, you can make donations to the GIRO account:

Community Revolving Loan Account, Account No. 52859403 Sort Code 72-00-01 at any Post Office, or send cheques payable to the above account, c/o Chrissie Schmidt, Redfield Community, Buckingham Road, Winslow, BUCKINGHAM, MK18 3LZ

For more books about communal living and holistic cultural change take a look at the Edge of Time website ...

www.edgeoftime.co.uk

CROSS INDEX KEY

GENERAL

adults = number of adults
children = number of children
open? = the community is open in principle to new members, although it may be full at present
charge? = community charges visitors to stay
volunteers? = community accepts volunteers

FOOD

meals? = there are regular communal meals
diet (dietry regime):

vgn = vegan
vtn = ovo-lacto-vegetarian

SPIRITUAL FOCUS (SPIRIT)

A = Anthroposophy (Philosophy of Rudolf Steiner)
B = Buddhist
C = Christian
H = Hindu
Q = Quaker
S = spiritual but non-specific
N = none

	location	adults	children	open?	charge?	volunteers?	meals?	diet	spirit	page
The Abbey	rural	6	0	●	●		●	vtn	S	30
Ashram	urban	60	12	●	●		●	vtn	C	32
Balnakeil	coastal	35	12	●	●				N	34
Beech Hill	rural	12	3	●			●	vtn	N	36
Bhaktivedanta	rural	50					●		H	38
Birchwood	rural	9	1				●		N	40
Blackcurrent	urban	5	2		●		●	vgn	N	42
Brambles	urban	7	0					vtn	N	44
Braziers	rural	10	1		●	●	●		N	46
Brithdir	rural	6	5	●	●	●	●		N	48
Brotherhood	rural			●				vtn	C	50
Brynderwen	semi-rural	3	0	●				vgn	N	52
Burton Bradstock	coastal	6		●	●				C	54
Camphill Schools	urban			●					A	56
Canon Frome	rural	26	17	●	●	●	●		N	58
CAT	rural	11	1		●	●			N	60
Clanabogan	rural	70	10	●					A	62
Community Proj	rural	37	33	●			●		N	64
Corani	urban	4	1	●					N	66
Cornerstone	urban	10						vtn	N	68
Coventry Peace	urban			●				vtn	N	70

Crabapple	rural	6	0	● ● ●	vtn	N	72
Createwel	rural	30	11	● ● ●	vgn		74
Darvell Bruderhof	rural	160	150	●		C	76
Earth Heart	rural	12	12				78
Earthworm	rural	6	3	● ● ●	vgn	N	80
Equinox	Urban	8	0	● ●	vgn	N	82
Erraid	rural	6	2	● ● ●		S	84
Faslane	rural			●		N	86
Findhorn	rural	135	15	● ● ●	vtn		88
Fireside	urban	8	4	● ● ●		S	90
Fox	rural	10	5	● ●	vgn	N	92
Frankleigh	rural	5	9	●		N	94
Gaunts	rural	40	0	● ● ●	vtn	S	96
Glyn Abbey	rural	17	8	● ●		N	98
Grimstone	rural	11	1	● ●		N	100
Gwerin	urban	21	1	●		N	102
Hargrave Rd	urban	10	2	●		N	104
Heartwood	rural	4	1	● ●	vtn	S	106
The Hive	urban	5	5	●		N	108
Hockerton	rural	9	11	● ●		N	110
Holy Rood	rural	4		● ●		N	112
Inverness L'Arche	urban	50	0	● ● ●		C	114
Keveral	rural	15	8	● ● ●		N	116
Lambeth L'Arche	urban	100	2	● ●		C	118

	location	adults	children	open?	charge?	volunteers?	meals?	diet	spirit	page
Land of Roots	rural	4	2	●			●		N	120
Laurieston	rural	22	6	●					N	122
Lee Abbey, Aston	urban	5		●			●		C	124
Liverpool L'Arche	urban	100	4	●			●		C	126
Loch Arthur	rural	65	10	●			●		A	128
Losang Dragpa	rural	30	3	●	●	●	●	vtn	B	130
Lothlorien	rural	12		●			●		B	132
Monimail	rural	5	2	●	●		●		N	134
Monkey Sanctuary	rural	9		●	●	●	●	vtn	N	136
Monkton Wyld	rural	12	0	●	●	●	●	vtn	N	138
Mornington Grove	urban	11	3	●	●		●	vtn	N	140
Neighbours	urban	8	7	●		●	●	vtn	C	142
New Education	semi-rural	3	1	●		●	●	vgn	N	144
New Futures	rural	42	14	●	●	●	●		N	146
Old Hall	rural	6	3	●		●	●		N	148
Parsonage	rural	40	30	●			●		N	150
Pennine	rural	50	3	●	●		●		A	152
Pilsdon	rural	3	2	●		●	●		C	154
Plants...future C	rural	3	2	●		●	●	vgn	N	156
Plants...future D	rural	2	0	●		●	●	vgn	N	158

Community										Page
Postlip	rural	18	11	●					N	160
Bamford Quaker	rural	12	8	●	●				Q	162
Rainbow	urban	34	20					vtn	N	164
Redfield	rural	15	7	●	●				N	166
Rubha Phoil	rural	4		●	●	●			N	168
Salisbury	urban							vtn	S	170
Sanford	urban								N	172
Shekinashram	semi-rural	5		●				vgn	S	174
Shrub Family	rural	6	4	●					N	176
Somefriends	urban	17		●				vtn	N	178
Springhill	urban	50	32	●	●			vtn	N	180
St Francis	rural	7		●					C	182
Stepping Stones	rural	7	4	●	●			vtn	N	184
Steward	rural	6	1	●				vgn	N	186
Talamh	rural	10	4			●		vtn	N	188
Tangram	urban	42	20	●	●				N	190
Taraloka	rural	12	0		●			vtn	B	192
Torch	urban	4					●		N	194
Townhead	rural	23	7	●	●			vtn	N	196
Tullycoll	rural	40	11	●					S	198
The Well	urban	7	5			●			C	200
Woodhead	rural	8	4	●	●			vtn	S	202
Woolman	urban	3	1			●			C	204
Zion	semi-rural	8		●				vgn	N	206

USEFUL CONTACTS

LEGAL STRUCTURE EXPERTS

Co-Operatives UK (formerly ICOM)
Hollyoak House, Hanover Street, Manchester, M60 0AS
Tel: 0161 46 959

Co-operative Development Agency (CDA)
To find your local CDA, contact Co-operatives UK. The CDA can set you up with model rules/Memorandum & Articles.

MONEY

Triodos Bank
Brunel House, 11 The Promenade, Clifton, Bristol, BS8 3NN
Tel: 0117 973 9339

Ecology Building Society
Belton Road, Silsden, Nr Keighley, West Yorkshire BD20 7EH
Tel: 01535 635933
info@ecology.co.uk

Radical Routes and **Rootstock**
See p 225

OTHER USEFUL ADDRESSES

The International Communal Studies Association (ICSA)
Yad Tabenkin, Ramat Efal 52960, Israel
Fax: +972 3 5346376
yadtab@actcom.co.il

In The Sticks
Market House, Market Place, Alston, Cumbria CA9 3HS
Tel: 01434 38680
http://www.inthesticks.com
A weekly newspaper full of advertisements for wierd and wonderful properties.

WWOOF UK
(worldwide opportunities on organic farms)
PO Box 2675, Lewes, East Sussex, BN7 1RB
Tel: 01273 476 286
email: hello@wwoof.org

We hope that you have found this edition of D&D to be both useful and enjoyable. We welcome feedback and invite you to fill out this postcard and return it to us.

What features did you like best about D&D 2004/2005?

What features would you add to a future edition?

What features would you leave out of a future edition?

How did you hear about Diggers & Dreamers?

Name
Address

Postcode
☐ We will continue to mail you about this and other publications distributed by Edge of Time unless you tick this box

Diggers&Dreamers
PUBLICATIONS

AFFIX
STAMP
HERE

Diggers & Dreamers
PUBLICATIONS

Diggers & Dreamers
BCM Edge
London
WC1N 3XX